ISLAND OF HOPE

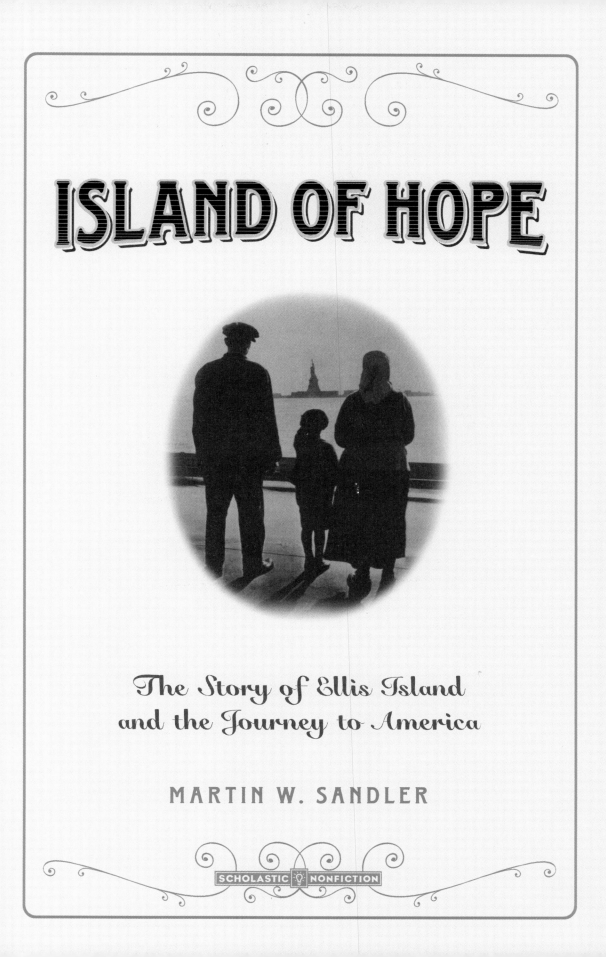

The Story of Ellis Island
and the Journey to America

MARTIN W. SANDLER

SCHOLASTIC NONFICTION

This book is dedicated to my grandfather Louis Sage who lived the immigrant experience and realized the immigrants' dream, and to all those who passed through Ellis Island and helped build a better America.

ACKNOWLEDGMENTS

I am most appreciative of the generous help given me by Barry Moreno, librarian and historian of the Ellis Island Immigration Museum. Thanks are also due to Barbara Puorro Galasso of the George Eastman House, Lyn Frederickson of Kansas State University, John Hallberg of the Institute for Regional Studies at North Dakota State University, Heather Morgan of Catholic University of America, Jack Naylor of the Naylor Museum of Photography, and Kia Campbell and Jesse Johnson of the Library of Congress.

As always, Carol W. Sandler has provided invaluable assistance. Finally, I am most indebted to Ken Wright, whose many suggestions inspired this book, and to Virginia "Ginny" Koeth and Danielle Denega, whose editorial skills and constant guidance shine through on every page.

Library of Congress Cataloging-in-Publication Data
Sandler, Martin W. Island of hope : the story of Ellis Island and the journey to America / Martin W. Sandler. p. cm. Summary: Relates the story of immigration to America through the voices and stories of those who passed through Ellis Island, from its opening in 1892 to the release of the last detainee in 1954. Includes bibliographical reference and index. Contents: America! America! – Island of Hope – Questions & Answers – Island of Tears – Starting New Lives – Building America. 1. Ellis Island Immigration Station (N.Y. and N.J.)—Juvenile literature. 2. United States—Emigration and immigration—History—Juvenile literature. [1. Ellis Island Immigration Station (N.Y. and N.J.)—History. 2. United States—Emigration and immigration—History. 3. Immigrants—History.] I. Title. JV6484.S36 2004 304.8'73—dc22 2003054448

All text and photo credits appear on pages 140–141.

0-439-53082-2

10 9 8 7 6 5 4 3 2 1   04 05 06 07 08

Printed in the U.S.A.   24
First printing, March 2004
Book design by Nancy Sabato Composition by Brad Walrod
Text is set in Lomba Book and Horndon.

CONTENTS

THE BOOK YOU ARE ABOUT TO READ tells the story of a very special place in the life of this nation. Located in New York Harbor within the shadow of the Statue of Liberty, it is named Ellis Island, and between 1892 and 1954, it served as the gateway to the United States for more than 12 million immigrants seeking to build new and better lives in America.

It was at Ellis Island's inspection facilities that millions of newcomers (as many as 3,000 to 5,000 a day) were required to undergo the physical, mental, and legal examinations that determined if they would be allowed to enter the land of opportunity they had heard so much about. No wonder many called it the Island of Hope.

Once there, however, some gave it a different name. They included the more than 250,000 who, having failed the inspections, suffered the worst fate of all: being sent back to their native countries. To all of these people, the more appropriate name for Ellis Island was Island of Tears. Fortunately, the vast majority passed the examinations and were, as one immigrant put it, "given our golden chance to be part of the promise of America."

Ellis Island was not the first immigration depot in the United States. From 1855 to 1890 some 8 million newcomers passed through the doors of the inspection station at Castle Island, located at the tip of Manhattan in New York City. And throughout the late 1800s and early 1900s other immigrants were processed at government stations at such ports as Boston, Massachusetts; Savannah, Georgia; Galveston Island, Texas; Locust Point in Baltimore, Maryland; and Angel Island in San Francisco, California.

But from the time that Ellis Island opened its doors on January 1, 1892, it became the primary receiving station for the greatest and most successful mass migration in modern history. Today some 100 million living Americans can trace their ancestry to those who passed through its halls.

I have chosen to tell most of the story of these immigrants through their own accounts. For it is their words that best reveal the dreams they shared, the risks they took, the dangers they encountered, and the challenges they faced in a strange new land. It is through their stories that we are reminded of how hard they worked to build a better America for us all.

A Polish immigrant, carrying all the belongings he could pack into one piece of luggage, prepares to board the ship that will take him to America. Ahead of him lay the long, often treacherous ocean voyage, the first of many challenges he would face.

CHAPTER 1

AMERICA! AMERICA!

"America was on everyone's lips. We talked about America; we dreamt about America. We all had one wish—to be in America." That is how a fifteen-year-old Polish boy named Louis Sage described his and his neighbors' feelings about what they had been told was a golden land far across the ocean. But Sage had also heard stories about a frightening place in America, a place called Ellis Island where all immigrants had to be examined before being allowed into the United States.

Many, he had been told, had failed these examinations and had been sent back to the country from which they had come.

Despite this concern, Louis Sage would come to America and would eventually prosper. What he could not know at the time was that in doing so he would be taking part in the greatest human migration in history, one in which more than 12 million others would share his Ellis Island experience.

There were almost as many reasons for coming to America as there were people who came. Most came to escape intolerable conditions in their homelands. In Ireland, a disease wiped out the potato crop upon which so many people depended, and more than a million people died of starvation. In other European countries years of drought led to similar situations. "We lived through a famine . . . [so] we came to America," explained one youngster. "My mother said she wanted to see a loaf of bread on the table and then she was ready to die."

As if these conditions were not harsh enough, there were other unbearable hardships as well. In many countries oppressive governments had eliminated freedom of speech, freedom of religion, and other time-honored legal rights. Many of these governments had begun to carry out massacres called pogroms, designed to eliminate minority groups, particularly Jews, who lived within their borders. "We had taken shelter in the attic of a house because a pogrom was raging in our town, and we were hiding from the mob," young Sophie Trupin later wrote. "My father at that time was in the cheese business . . . and he had his long cheese knife. He decided that before he and his family were killed he would kill as many of the attackers as he possibly could. It was

Years of crop failure forced many Irish to abandon their homes and seek a new life in the United States. "In many places," a visiting American priest observed, "the wretched people were seated on the fences of their decaying gardens, wringing their hands and wailing bitterly the destruction that had left them foodless."

up in that attic, surrounded by his terrified family, that my father vowed that he would leave this accursed Russia and make a new life for himself and his family in America."

Given all these horrors, it was not surprising that so many risked everything to seek a new life in a strange land. As one Italian immigrant explained, "If America did not exist, we would have had to invent it for the sake of our survival."

Actually, it was not survival alone that drew the immigrants to the New World. While millions of people were pushed out of their countries by unlivable situations, millions of others were pulled out of their native lands by the promise of America. By the late 1800s, the United States had achieved a worldwide reputation as a nation offering

For those who, like this Norwegian woman, decided to emigrate to America, saying farewell was one of the most difficult experiences of their lives. Most left their homeland knowing that they would never see their parents or their village again.

personal freedom and unlimited opportunity. European newspapers were filled with accounts that portrayed America as the "golden land." Somewhere across the ocean was a place where all could travel around and worship as they pleased. There were no pogroms. Anyone could get rich.

Letters to relatives and friends from earlier emigrants told of tables groaning with food and stores flowing with clothing and goods beyond description. Steamship companies, anxious to lure as many passengers as possible, distributed posters and handbills throughout Europe describing the vast acres of land and the wide variety of jobs that were to be had. Not all the immigrants were convinced that these claims were true. But as conditions continued to get worse, even the most doubtful came to believe that life had to be better in America. So to America they came—the poor, the oppressed, the hopeful. Each had his own dream and the courage to leave all that was familiar behind to enter a world of unknowns. Few could anticipate the challenges they would be forced to face.

The first of these challenges was saying good-bye to relatives and friends. "I can remember only the hustle and bustle of those last weeks in Pinsk, the farewells from the family, the embraces and the tears," Russian immigrant Golda Meir later recalled. "Going to America then was almost like going to the moon. . . . We were all bound for places about which we knew nothing at all and for a country that was totally strange to us."

Most of the immigrants lived in remote areas, and the trip to the nearest port from which ships bound for America departed was the first major journey of their lives. Some traveled by wagon, others on donkey or even on foot. Those who could scrape together the fare and who lived relatively close to a railroad line made the journey

Even though the average cost of a steerage ticket was only $30, the steamship companies that brought the immigrants to America made enormous profits. The larger steamships could hold from 1,500 to 2,000 immigrants and earned their owners some $60,000 in profits for a single, one-way voyage.

by train. Many of the most poignant farewells took place at the railroad depots. "My father," an Italian immigrant remembered, "put my valises (suitcases) on the old mule, Old Titi, and we went up to the railroad station. It was pitch dark, early in the morning. From the cracks in the shutters over here and over there I could see the yellow light of the oil

THE RANKS OF PEOPLE who made vital contributions to their country and to the world are filled with hundreds whose life journeys included passing through Ellis Island. One of the most shining examples is Golda Meir, the young Russian-Jewish immigrant who felt that "going to America then was like going to the moon." After surviving the Ellis Island ordeal, Meir and her family settled in Milwaukee, Wisconsin. While in high school she became very interested in the attempts to create an independent Jewish nation. In 1921 she and her husband moved to Tel Aviv in what was then Palestine in order to take an active part in these efforts.

When Israel gained status as an independent nation in 1948, Meir was appointed the country's ambassador to the Soviet Union. A year later she became Israel's foreign minister, a post she held until 1966. Then, in 1969, she was elected prime minister. It marked only the second time in history that a woman had been elected to head a nation (the first being Sirimavo Bandaranaike of Sri Lanka).

As the leader of Israel, Golda Meir had many important achievements, including the way she cemented relationships with the United States and the emerging independent nations of Africa. Perhaps most notable was her success opening Israel's doors to people from around the world, an accomplishment undoubtedly inspired by the opportunities presented to her as an immigrant to the United States.

lamps. The streets were empty. I could smell the air like when the hay is damp. . . . My father did not speak all the way to the train. I don't know when he said it to me, my father, he said, 'Make yourself courage.' And that was the last time I saw my father."

Often, when they finally reached the port, the travelers would have to wait days or even weeks for their ship to arrive. When the vessel, belching steam, did appear, most were awestruck. The vast majority had never seen a ship before.

On the docks, before boarding the vessels that would take them to America, the immigrants were subjected to the first of many inspections. In order to get the right to transport newcomers to the United States, European steamship companies had to agree that if an immigrant failed the Ellis Island examinations, the company would transport that person, free of charge, back to the country from which he or she had come. Because of this, steamship authorities were as careful as they could be not to let anyone aboard who was likely to be sent back.

The immigrants were surrounded by steamship-line doctors. After being vaccinated and disinfected, they were turned over to other steamship officials, who put them through a barrage of twenty-nine questions. What is your name? Your age? Your nationality? Your occupation? Where did you last live? they were asked. What is your mental and physical health? Can you read and write? Do you have at least twenty-five dollars with you? Have you ever been in prison? Are you married? Do you have more than one husband or wife? Are you a foe (enemy) of government?

All of the answers to these and other questions were recorded on sheets of paper called manifests. Although the immigrants did not know it, the manifests would be important to their future. The information that the travelers supplied would play a significant role in helping officials decide whether the immigrants would be allowed to enter America or be put on the next ship back to their native lands.

Once the questioning on the docks was over, the passengers were led up the gangplank and onto the ship. Many had heard stories of the harrowing ocean voyage and were gripped with fear. Others, however, had only their destination in mind. "So at last I was going to America, really, really going at last!" wrote a Jewish girl named Mary Antin. "The boundaries burst. The arch of heaven soared. A million suns shone out for every star. The winds rushed in from outer space, roaring in my ears. America, America."

The departure from the port was often as heart-wrenching as the farewells at the villages had been. One type of send-off in particular would always be remembered by those who witnessed it. "Many immigrants," wrote Italian passenger Luciano DeCrescenzo, "had brought onboard balls of yarn, leaving one end of the line with someone on land. As the ship slowly cleared the dock, the balls unwound amid the farewell shouts of the women, the fluttering of the handkerchiefs, and the infants held high. After the yarn ran out, the long strips remained airborne, sustained by the wind, long after those on land and those at sea had lost sight of each other."

Once the ship was out of sight of land, the passengers turned their attention to the quarters that would be their home for the next ten

Thousands of females came to America after having their passage paid for by men anxious to find a wife. This young woman was particularly fortunate, since the fiancé she had never seen or met had sent her a first-class ticket, allowing her to escape the horrible conditions commonly encountered in steerage.

days to more than a month, depending on the speed of the vessel and the weather it encountered. For those wealthy enough to have purchased first- or second-class tickets, getting used to life on the sea was relatively easy. Those in first- or second-class had rooms to themselves with comfortable beds, clean fresh water, toilet and bathing facilities, and even fireplaces. At mealtime, they could choose from a rich and varied menu. Between meals, they had the freedom of the open deck. "The S.S. *Baltic* was beautiful," recalled first-class passenger Martha O'Flanagan. "I didn't want to get off . . . because I loved the blue waters

On calm days, steerage passengers were allowed to escape the foul air of their quarters by going up to what was called the steerage deck. Still, the steerage experience was one that no immigrant would ever forget.

. . . I was with another girl and her brother and her sister. The four of us traveled together from Ireland to the United States. She [the other girl] had been [in America] ten years and she had gone home on a visit to see her family, and now she was returning. We used to . . . dance all the Irish dances up on deck. We had a great time."

The vast majority of the immigrants, however, had anything but a great time. Far too poor to afford first- or second-class tickets, they were herded together in the dim, damp section called steerage that was far below the decks. The accommodations there were horrendous.

"The unattended vomit of the seasick, the odors of not-too-clean bodies, the reek of food, and the awful stench of the nearby toilet rooms

make the atmosphere in steerage such that it is a marvel that human flesh can endure it," exclaimed one government report. "Most immigrants lie in their berths for most of the voyage, in a stupor caused by the foul air. The food often repels them. . . . It is almost impossible to keep personally clean. All of these conditions are naturally aggravated by the crowding."

The accommodations in first class and steerage were worlds apart. But, aside from their dream of America, there was another thing all the passengers had in common. That was the fierce ocean storms that the ships inevitably encountered on their way across the Atlantic.

Remembering one of the storms, a Balkan immigrant wrote of "the howling darkness, the white rims of the mountain-high waves

Famed American photographer Alfred Stieglitz took this photograph of men, women, and children aboard the steamship that brought them to America. Between 1880 and 1920, so many immigrants came to the United States that their numbers in each decade were far larger than the entire population of the nation in 1776.

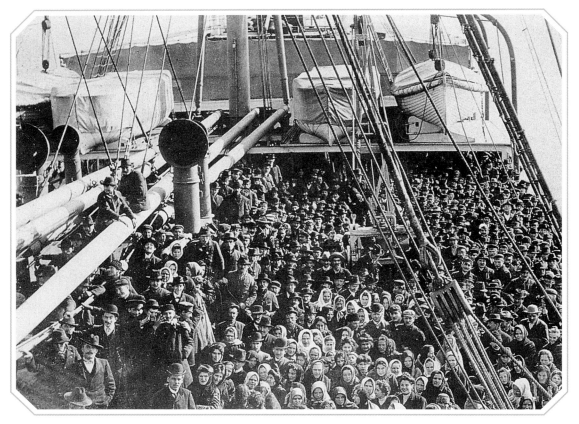

Many native-born Americans regarded the enormous flow of immigrants with alarm.
Others welcomed their entry. "Let them all come," wrote author/philosopher Ralph
Waldo Emerson, "The energy of Irish, Germans, Swedes, Poles . . . and all the European
tribes . . . will construct a new race, a new religion, a new state, a new literature."

speeding like maddened dragons toward the tumbling ship...." Bertha
Devlin, a young Irish immigrant, had her own terrifying experience.
"Oh, God, I was sick," she recalled. "Everybody was sick. I don't ever
want to remember anything about that old boat. One night I prayed
to God that it would go down because the waves were washing over
it. I was that sick, I didn't care if it went down or not. And everybody
else was the same way."

Although she was only five years old when she sailed to America
aboard the *Campania,* Agnes Howerbend had one memory of the voy-

age that stayed with her all her life. "The storm was so great," she recalled. "Two people had died. I don't know how they did. But I well remember Father at the funeral on deck, each one of us in hand. I turned around and they were throwing caskets overboard into the ocean . . . I remember that vividly."

Finally, after all the days, and even weeks, at sea, after all the hardships of steerage and weather, the immigrant ships would approach New York Harbor. "My first impressions of the New World will always remain etched in my memory, particularly that hazy October morning when I first saw Ellis Island," Italian immigrant Edward Corsi would later write. "The steamer *Florida*, 14 days out of Naples, filled to capacity with 1,600 natives of Italy, had weathered one of the worst storms in our captain's memory. . . . My mother, my stepfather, my brother, Giuseppe, and my two sisters, Liberta and Helvetia, all of us together, happy that we had come through the storm safely, clustered on the foredeck for fear of separation and looked with wonder on this miraculous land of our dreams."

They were almost there—but not quite. Instead of heading directly for Ellis Island, the ships, now pulled by powerful tugboats, made their way into the lower bay of New York Harbor. There the ships dropped anchor and the passengers were forced to wait until government doctors could examine the new arrivals.

Often, there were so many immigrant ships in the bay that the newcomers had to wait days before the doctors were ready to board their vessel and begin their examinations. Italian immigrant Angelina Palmiero remembered how, for her, the delay was made a bit less maddening. "We docked in the harbor," she recalled. "Ellis Island was too crowded. There were quite a few boats from other ports. Each boat had to wait their turn. I don't remember how many days we anchored, but it was quite a few days because my father used to come with the tugboat. And that's how I saw him for the first time, from all the way up on the railing, looking down. I remember he bought big bananas from vendors on the tugboat. They would put the bananas in a pail and lift it up to the ship. I didn't know what bananas were. 'Don't eat it like that,' he shouted. 'Take the skin off.'"

When the doctors finally were able to come aboard, they checked the immigrants for such contagious diseases as smallpox, yellow fever, and measles. Those found to be infected were taken off the vessels and transferred to hospitals. The inspections were difficult enough. But while they were being conducted, the immigrants learned a painful lesson as well. It was here that they got their first hint that while America might be the land of freedom of which they had dreamed, it might not be a land of full equality. For it quickly became clear that the first- and second-class passengers were not being put through the physical examinations. Instead, they were being told that once the ship got under way again and docked at a pier in New York, they would be free to enter America. They would not have to endure what lay ahead for most of the new arrivals at Ellis Island. "There was this slight feeling among us," recalled one steerage passenger, "that, isn't it strange that here we are coming to a country where there is complete equality, but not quite so for the newly arrived immigrants."

Once the shipboard examinations were completed, the vessel

THE STATUE OF LIBERTY was a gift from the people of France to the people of the United States as a symbol of the two nations' commitment to the principles of liberty. Created by Frederic Auguste Bartholdi, it took more than twelve years to finish work on the monument.

The statue was finally completed in 1884 and stood on display in France for a year. In 1885 it was dismantled and sent to New York in 214 enormous packing crates. It was then reassembled and placed on a 65-foot-high granite pedestal on Bedloe's Island in New York Harbor. The pedestal was funded in great measure by thousands of small donations from schoolchildren throughout the United States.

Inscribed on the statue's pedestal was a poem titled "The New Colossus," written by Jewish immigrant Emma Lazurus. Included in the now-famous poem are the lines:

> *Give me your tired, your poor,*
> *Your huddled masses yearning to breathe free,*
> *The wretched refuse of your teeming shore.*
> *Send these, the homeless, tempest-tossed to me,*
> *I lift my lamp beside the golden door!*

Today, some 120 years after they were written, these words still ring true. The Statue of Liberty remains one of our proudest symbols, reflecting the hopes of all those who still come to America seeking freedom and opportunity.

began the last short leg of its voyage. As it approached the piers of Manhattan, the first of what would be many amazing sights came into view. It was the Statue of Liberty. Some of the newcomers had read about the statue in school and knew what it was. Most had not. "When we arrived in New York Harbor, my brothers and I ran out to see the Statue of Liberty," recalled German immigrant Estelle Miller. "One man said, 'Don't you know? That's Columbus.'"

To some, however, the statue was the inspirational symbol that its creator had intended it to be. "I saw the Statue of Liberty," stated Greek immigrant Doukanie Papandreos, "and I said to myself, 'Lady, you're beautiful. You opened your arms and you get all the foreigners here. Give me a chance to prove that I am worth it, to do something to become somebody in America . . . .'"

Whether they understood the towering statue's meaning or not, none would ever forget the sight. "I thought she was one of the seven wonders of the world," exclaimed a German newcomer.

"The bigness of Mrs. Liberty overcame us," a Polish immigrant would later write. "No one spoke a word, for she was a goddess and we knew she represented the big, powerful country which was to be our future home."

About half a mile beyond the statue was another sight: the vast complex of redbrick buildings that stood upon Ellis Island. But the immigrants still were not yet there. Slowly their vessel pulled into one of the Manhattan piers. With their legs still shaking from their long days aboard ship, the immigrants were at last allowed to disembark. On the dock, while the first- and second-class passengers

"When I saw the Statue of Liberty . . . it was something beautiful,"
fourteen-year-old Italian immigrant Victor Tartarini later
recalled. "I knew I was in America . . . I knew I was going to see
my father . . . I had somebody to love."

Ellis Island's Main Building is a handsome structure featuring picturesque towers, delicate limestone trim, and copper domes. Many immigrants would find it ironic that traumatic experiences took place in such a beautiful setting.

were being released, the steerage passengers were assembled into groups of thirty. Then, they and their baggage—clothing, feather beds, family bibles, photographs, and other mementos of their native lands—were loaded on barges for the short trip to Ellis Island.

As the crowded barges neared the island, the city of New York came into full view. Here the newcomers were confronted with yet another amazing new sight: the skyscrapers that towered above the city. "Mountains! Look at them!" exclaimed an Italian boy. "Why don't they have snow on them?" For many of the arrivals, the most awesome sight of all was Ellis Island's Main Building. "I never saw such a big building—the size of it," stated Russian newcomer Celia Adler. "According to the houses I left in my town, this was like a whole city in one, in one building. It was an enormous thing to see, I tell you."

It may have been "an enormous thing to see," but it was a frightening first encounter as well. "I was always afraid of Ellis Island," Scottish immigrant Marge Glasgow later reported. "I had heard stories that if they keep you at Ellis Island, they go through your hair looking for bugs. My mother was always scaring me with that."

Most were not only frightened; they were confused as well. As soon as the barges landed, the immigrants were greeted by uniformed men speaking a language few of them could understand. "When we got to Ellis Island," stated English arrival Eleanor Lenhart, "they put the gangplank down and there was a man at the foot, and he was shouting at the top of his voice, 'Put your luggage here, drop your luggage here. Men this way. Women and children this way.' Dad looked at us and said, 'We'll meet you back here at this mound of luggage and hope we find it and you again and see you later.'"

They had come from many different countries. Each had his or her own reason for coming. But they had shared many things as well: the difficult ocean voyage, the fear of the unknown, and most of all, the dream of freedom in America. Now they were about to share another experience they would never forget—Ellis Island and the ordeal that would decide whether or not their dream would become a reality.

Many new arrivals had no idea what took place at Ellis Island. Others had heard what was in store for them. "We knew what we were coming to," Ukrainian immigrant Fannie Friedman explained. "That you have to stay there. And that they're going to examine you again and again. . . . We knew this is the way to come to this wonderful land."

CHAPTER 2

ISLAND OF HOPE

"Ellis Island—you got thousands of people marching in, a little bit excited, a little bit scared. Just imagine you're 14½ years old and you're in a strange country and you don't know what's going to happen." That's how Albert Mardirossian, a young Armenian immigrant, remembered feeling as he stepped through the gates of the massive inspection station. Like all those who would pass through the Island, Mardirossian had been led from the dock to the Main Building. It was a strange sight:

hundreds, even thousands, of foreigners, most dressed in their native attire, marching along with numbered tags pinned to their caps and clothing, their hands filled with small parcels or bundles. "We had all sorts of tags on us," recalled Hungarian arrival Anne Vida. "We must have looked like marked-down merchandise at [a department store]."

To some, the tags themselves were bewildering. "They put tags on us," Romanian newcomer Carl Belapp later reported. "My tag said 'E.I.' Other tags said something else....What is E.I.? Am I considered a criminal? Then I found out what E.I. stands for: Ellis Island."

Newly arrived immigrants, small luggage in hand, mount the stairs leading to the Registry Room. The photographer who took this picture titled it "Climbing into America."

When the immigrants reached the Main Building, they were directed to the steep stairway leading to the Registry Room, where the inspections would take place. As they climbed the stairs, three abreast, they became aware of uniformed men standing at both the foot and the top of the stairway. To many, the fact that these onlookers were in uniform caused immediate alarm. "I had run away from

THE FIRST TO ENTER

ON JANUARY 1, 1892, the steamship *Nevada*, filled with European immigrants hoping to build a new life in America, entered New York Harbor. Aboard the vessel was Annie Moore, a fifteen-year-old girl from Ireland. As the *Nevada* neared the new immigrant inspection station at Ellis Island, Moore and her fellow passengers were greeted with the sound of scores of bells and whistles. Few of them were aware that this was the station's opening day and that the sounds they were hearing were in celebration of the occasion.

By chance, Annie Moore was the first to be let off the ship and to be led into Ellis Island's Main Building. Already fearful of what lay ahead, she became even more frightened when she was immediately surrounded by a horde of uniformed men and reporters. Her eyes grew even wider when one of the officials suddenly put a shiny ten-dollar gold piece in her hand. Then he told her that the gift was because she was the first immigrant to enter the new inspection station.

Annie Moore would successfully undergo her Ellis Island examinations and would be allowed to enter America. She would first live in New York City, eventually get married, and then, with her husband and children, finally settle in the American West. She would have many memories of her life in the Old World and the New. Most of all, she would remember the day when she not only stepped into a new country but into history as well.

uniforms," Louis Sage later recalled. "My reason for coming to America was that uniformed men had forced my brothers into the terrible Russian army. Then, even though I was only fifteen, they came looking for me. The sight of all those uniforms at Ellis Island, I'll tell you, was terrifying."

What neither Sage nor any of the other newcomers knew was that the uniformed men were not merely onlookers but doctors, and that the inspection process had already begun. As the immigrants made their way up the stairs, the doctors watched them closely, checking for any obvious signs of infirmities, illnesses, or mental oddities. Was the newcomer breathing heavily as he made the steep climb? Was he limping? Was he coughing or wheezing? Were there any other signs of a physical or mental disorder that would keep that person from finding a job in the United States, making him unable to support himself?

Even the children did not escape this initial scrutiny. Those older than two years were taken from their mothers' arms. Doctors watched them walk to make sure they were not crippled. Children were also asked to state their names to prove that they were not deaf or mute.

If one of the doctors suspected that something might be wrong with a newcomer, that person's clothing was marked in chalk with a symbol standing for a particular disorder. The symbols included L for lameness, H for suspected heart disease, E for eye problems, and Ft for feet. Those suspected of having mental disabilities were chalked with an X. Once the formal inspections began, other doctors would pay special attention to the chalk marks. Years later most of the immigrants, even those who had passed through Ellis Island without major incident, would recall the look on the faces of those whose clothing had been marked with the dreaded chalk.

When the immigrants reached the top of the stairway, they were led into the Registry Room, also called the Great Hall. Most had never been in such an enormous room, larger even than the town squares in the villages from which they had come. They were also startled by the long rows of heavy iron railings that had been erected to help move them along in an orderly fashion as they were being examined. The railings gave the room

As they awaited their examinations, many of the newcomers were startled by the appearance of some of their fellow immigrants. Here, newly arrived Russian Cossacks pose for a photographer.

a jaillike appearance, and many of the newcomers had come from countries where being put in jail for the most trivial reasons was all too common. "Why should they put us in jail?" Polish arrival Clara Rudder remembered thinking. "We didn't do anything wrong."

Along with this concern was the trauma of having to wait once again before one's fate was decided. Yugoslavian arrival Ljubica

"So many of those who had arrived on other ships," Polish immigrant Louis Sage later stated, "looked so different from the people we had seen all our lives back home." This Greek soldier arrived wearing a military uniform.

Wuchina remembered "The big room packed with people, surging with people." Thomas Rogen, an Irish immigrant, had his own recollections. "The one thing I remember about Ellis Island was confusion," he later stated. "A lot of movement and people, women wearing babushkas, [lots of] kerchiefs and boxes and bundles. I remember officers, officials with blue coats and brass buttons going back and forth. Rows of benches in a big hall with kids running in all directions. . . ."

And there was the noise. In the Registry Room all the languages of the world seemed to cry out at once. The sound was deafening. Shouts like "I'm over here" or "Be quiet, child" rang out in Italian, Greek, Russian, French, German, and a dozen other languages. Most of the immigrants, particularly the youngsters, had never seen people from other nations, or even villages. The sight of all these different types of people with strange clothing and mannerisms was bewildering.

Some of the immigrants had left their native lands when the weather was much different than when they arrived in New York Harbor. Emmanuel Steen, a young man from Ireland, was one of them.

"That day," he recalled, "there must have been three, four ships. Maybe five, six thousand people. Jammed! And remember, it was August. Hot as a pistol, and I'm wearing my long johns and a heavy Irish tweed suit. Got my overcoat on my arm. It was the beginning of fall back home, see. And I'm carrying my suitcase. I'm dying with the heat. I never experienced such heat. During the day, that hall became so hot, and all they had was a couple of rotating fans, which did nothing except raise the dust. I just wanted to get . . . out of there."

Newly arrived immigrants wait for their names to be called so their examinations can begin. "I was afraid," recalled one newcomer, "that I would miss my name and remain there forever."

Getting out of there was on almost everyone's mind. But even if everything went without serious incident, undergoing all the physical, mental, and legal examinations that lay ahead could take up to five or six hours. For some, however, the time between inspections was made a bit easier by surprising new encounters. "What I remember most about Ellis Island," stated one new arrival, "was that for the first time in my life I did not see any religious pictures on the walls." Lithuanian immigrant Rita Seltzer even had a humorous experience. "Coming to a strange, strange country, everybody's strange to you . . . I remember standing [in the Registry Room] and looking up to the balcony. There were a lot of people standing and chewing. I was thinking to myself, 'What is that? Is there a sickness here? They all keep chewing.' Until I talked to my family later, they explained to me that this was chewing gum. Nobody's sick."

When they arrived at Ellis Island, many of the immigrants had gone a long time without food. Given something to eat, some discovered a strange new treat. "I remember the first meal they gave to us at Ellis Island," Italian arrival Peter Mossini later stated. "They gave a sandwich—white bread with a piece of cheese and a piece of ham—and it tasted so good. It tasted like a nice piece of cake. That was something new for me. I [had] never seen sandwiches in Sicily."

Finally, almost unexpectedly, an immigrant would hear his or her name called out. It was time for the formal medical inspections to begin. One of the first was the hair inspection, the prospect of which had frightened young Marge Glasgow long before she got to America. "They examined if you had lice in your head," recalled Peter Mossini.

"If you did, they shaved your hair. I remember that there [were] a lot of bald people."

Another examination was for skin disease. Since bathing aboard the ships had been almost impossible, many groups were made to bathe with disinfectant solutions before the skin examinations began. Once the exams started, many of the newcomers were forced to take off some of their clothes. German immigrant John Peter was only five years old

"In the week before we left Romania," 15-year-old Selma Krames later stated, "I had a terrible cough that got worse on the damp trip over. I was terrified that they would find something wrong and send me back."

when he stood beside his mother while she was being examined. "All the ladies there were stripped down to the waist," he recalled, "and this made me ask many questions to my mother, [like] how come all these women stripped down to the waist and looked like that. I'd never seen a woman stripped before."

For women in particular, the examination for skin disease was but one of several physical inspections that would prove to be particularly difficult. Until 1914, well after the greatest flow of immigrants to

America had taken place, all of the Ellis Island doctors were men. For a woman who had never been touched by a man other than her husband, being examined by a male doctor was humiliating. But it was not only women who were put through humiliating experiences. "I had to open my trousers and fly and they checked me for venereal disease or hernia or whatever they were looking for," recalled Emmanuel Steen. "I was in good shape, you know, but just the same I felt this was very demeaning, even then. I mean, it's terrible with women, young girls, and everyone you know. And we had to line up in front of them. . . . Years later I thought they didn't have to do it that way. But this was the height of immigration. We were coming in by the thousands. . . ."

They were indeed coming in by the thousands, and in their need to process so many people, the doctors were sometimes mistaken in their initial observations. "We had a very peculiar experience," remembered Palestinian newcomer Rachel Chenitz. "When we were in Le Havre [Holland], my older sister decided to buy my mother a nice pair of shoes. So, they had . . . heels. My mother was never accustomed to heels [and she walked very funny in the shoes] . . . they [noticed this and] started to look at her feet and test her. They were going to send us back because they thought [that because of the way she walked in the shoes] something was wrong with her." Fortunately, with the aid of an interpreter, Chenitz's family was able to convince the doctors that the problem was with her shoes, not her feet, and the mother and the rest of the family were passed on to the next inspection.

Given what was at stake, all of the physical inspections were frightening. But most terrifying of all was the eye examination, during which the immigrants were checked to see if they had an eye disease called trachoma. It was a terrible infirmity that often resulted in blindness. And it was highly contagious as well.

The great flow of immigration took place at a time when trachoma was spreading throughout southern and eastern Europe. Because of this, and the dire consequences of the disease, trachoma, more than any other illness that the immigrants might bring with them, was what immigration officials feared most. So much so that the United States commissioner general of immigration had publicly warned that if trachoma was allowed to enter the United States through the newcomers, future Americans would be rendered "sightless" and the United States would become "the hospital of the nations of the world."

Back in the old country some of the arrivals had heard that having something wrong with their eyes was one of the main reasons for people being sent back home. "There were many people in our neighborhood who could not read or write, and they had relatives in America, so they came to my mother that she should read their letters," Polish immigrant Isaac Bashevis Singer would later write. "And they all wrote about . . . how they came to America . . . and they also wrote about Ellis Island, which they called the Island of Tears, and about all the troubles some of the immigrants had when they came. There was [such] a great fear of this island [that] many immigrants, I remember, [tried] to cure their eyes . . . which they suspected might hinder them of entering the United States."

Other immigrants, while unaware that trachoma was almost a certain cause for being sent back, had heard terrible stories about the eye

ISAAC BASHEVIS SINGER, whose mother had helped her neighbors by translating the letters they received from relatives in America, came to the United States in 1935 to escape the bitter anti-Semitism that surrounded him in his native Poland. Unlike most of his fellow immigrants, Singer had enjoyed a measure of success in the Old World, both as an editor and a writer. It was in America, however, that his literary career blossomed.

Before this career was over, Singer would establish himself as one of the world's most respected authors. A tireless worker, he wrote more than forty novels, short stories, plays, and essays. Each was characterized by Singer's memories of his Jewish heritage and his Old World experiences. He wrote all his works in Yiddish, which was then translated into English. The chief subject of his novels in particular was traditional Jewish-Polish life in various periods of history. Not surprising given his own life history, the central theme of these books was the conflict expressed by those who sought to preserve old ways of life after having moved to new and strange surroundings in America.

Despite the serious nature of his work, Singer was, above all, a marvelous storyteller. It was a talent that enabled him to write several compelling children's books filled with fantasy and superstition. By the time he died in 1991, Singer had become one of the most honored of all writers. His many literary awards included two National Book Awards and the Nobel Prize for literature.

examination itself. "I remember when I got on the boat," young Italian immigrant Amelia Giacomo recounted, "my mother took a liking to this gentleman because he was so knowledge-able about Ellis Island. We knew you could be deported [sent back] or detained if something was wrong with you. . . . Well, one day, we took a walk on the boat. I was

The eye examination was commonly the last of the physical inspections. The worried looks on the faces of these immigrants reflect their fear in knowing that should they be found to have trachoma, they would immediately be deported.

only five years old. And [the man] said, 'You know what? When you get over to Ellis Island they're going to examine your eyes with a hook,' and he says, 'Don't let them do it because you know what? They did it to me—one eye fell in my pocket.'"

The man was joking, of course, but his reference to the hook was all too true. When, with trembling limbs, the immigrants stood before Ellis Island doctors for their eye examination, they were first asked to read the words on an identification card so that the doctors could see if their eyes were focusing correctly. Then the doctor tilted the new-comer's head and snapped back the person's upper eyelids with a curved instrument. Most often the instrument was a buttonhook, the same metal device that fashionable ladies used to button up their shoes or long gloves. No wonder the eye doctors were often referred to as the "buttonhook men."

Throughout all the examinations, doctors paid special attention to those whose clothing bore a chalk mark, placed there when they had first climbed the stairs to the Registry Room. If the more thorough examination revealed that the immigrant did indeed show signs of the infirmity indicated by the chalk mark, or if a doctor now put his own chalk mark on the immigrant's clothing, that person would be separated from their family and would be detained for further physical examination or sent to the Ellis Island hospital.

The distress caused by such separations was heart-wrenching to all who observed them. "Next to me," recalled Greek immigrant Doukanie Papandreos, "was an Italian woman with three children, and one of the children got sick. Pneumonia, I think it was. . . . The mother was holding the child and singing. All of a sudden, a doctor and two nurses took the child away. The mother couldn't speak English. And they're talking to her in English. They were saying that the child had to go to the hospital. And they took the child from her arms, and the mother was crying, and I was crying for her, too. I was praying so hard for her, for me."

The vast majority of newcomers did not suffer such trauma. Despite all they had to go through, most were not detained for medical reasons. But, as their medical cards were stamped PASSED, they could look ahead of them to the far end of the Registry Room. There, standing behind tall desks, a whole new squadron of inspectors was waiting to put them through mental and legal examinations that could be even more trying than the physical inspections. For the immigrants, the Ellis Island ordeal was far from over.

Photographers used their cameras to record almost every aspect of the Ellis Island experience. Photographer Lewis Hine titled this picture of a mother and her children "Mona Lisa Madonna."

Immigrants line up waiting to be called for their mental and legal examinations. For many, these inspections would be more trying and more potentially disastrous than the physical examinations had been.

CHAPTER 3

QUESTIONS & ANSWERS

"He asked me a lot of silly questions," stated English immigrant Florence Norris. "You know what I mean? About America, if I knew all about America. Well, I didn't know anything about America." Neither did most of the other newcomers, but they were expected to answer this question and many others.

Immigrants who had passed their physical tests were herded together in front of a doorway leading to a large area containing fenced-off aisles and booths. The scene was vividly described by a writer for *Harper's Weekly* magazine. "Presently there is a stir," wrote the reporter. "A waiting figure stands before the little desk at the end of each lane; every booth is [manned]; interpreters mass themselves; and there is the distant clatter of many feet as the immigrants crowd openmouthed and bewildered through the . . . doorway. For a moment all is confusion; the carefully ticketed groups are broken, as friends find themselves separated or parents see their little ones stupidly assigned to another batch. At length they come down their proper lanes in single file, their queer baggage bumping against the rails and playing havoc with those in the rear. They clearly have no notion of what is to follow. Some look frightened when halted at the desks, some angry, and some show little emotion. . . . Many are nervously defiant; now and again a woman's laugh sounds perilously akin to hysteria."

Many of the immigrants had been warned that the mental and legal examinations were often even more trying than the physical inspections, particularly the many questions they would be asked during the legal queries. As some approached the new set of inspectors, they feverishly rehearsed answers to questions they had been warned about: Where are you going? Have you been in prison? Do you have money? Do you have a job waiting? But these questions would come later. First came the mental tests.

As the immigrants entered the booths where the examiners were seated, the inspectors studied their faces and movements for obvious signs of mental disorder. Then, since so many of the arrivals could neither read nor write, they were asked to solve a simple arithmetic problem, such as counting backward from twenty. Finally, they were given equally simple puzzles to solve. These included completing a half-drawn face, drawing a happy face and a sad face, drawing a circle or a diamond. Some were given wooden blocks and asked to arrange them in certain ways. Those who, in the judgment of the inspectors, did not perform adequately, had an *X* put on their clothing in chalk, signifying that they were to be detained for further mental examination.

Those immigrants passing through Ellis Island after 1917 were forced to take an additional mental test. By this time, so many

An immigrant attempts to solve a puzzle during her mental examination. The inspector checks his stopwatch to determine if she can complete the test within the time allowed.

HELP WAS AT HAND

WITH THE OPENING OF ELLIS ISLAND and the beginning of the greatest influx of foreigners that any nation had ever experienced, the services provided by emigrant aid societies, the earliest of which were established in colonial days, became more important than ever. They became so valuable and were in such great demand, in fact, that organizations such as the Hebrew Immigration Aid Society, the Society for Italian Immigrants, the Austrian Society, and the Association for the Protection of Belgian and Dutch Immigrants, to name but a few, established offices within Ellis Island itself. This allowed them to be constantly available to immigrants in need.

The needs were many. The services provided by the aid societies ranged from helping Ellis Island interpreters and inspectors communicate with the immigrants, to providing temporary shelter for thousands who had been released from the Island. Society workers also proved invaluable in directing newcomers to legitimate employers. They spent days, even weeks, writing letters and sending telegrams seeking to find missing relatives and others for whom immigrants were waiting. Often they accompanied those who had been detained when they went before the dreaded Board of Inquiry. And throughout the immigrants' entire Ellis Island experience, they provided comfort to men, women, and children who were going through what, for many, was the most terrifying time of their lives.

immigrants had poured into America that Congress had passed a law requiring that all newcomers sixteen years and older had to be able to read a forty-word passage in their native language or they would not be able to enter the United States. This new requirement was often met with resourcefulness on the part of those being tested and their families. Young Armenian immigrant Helen Saban was a member of one such family. "[Since my mother] didn't know English," Saban recalled, "my uncle Leon interpreted for her. Immigration officials asked whether or not she read Armenian. Uncle Leon said to her, 'Say yes.' She said [to him] in Armenian, 'But I don't know.' He said, 'You just say yes.' She said, 'Yes.' They handed her a book in Armenian. She said to my uncle, 'Now what do I do?' He says, in Armenian, of course . . . 'Open a page and recite the Lord's Prayer in Armenian.' So she did. As soon as she did that, they passed her."

Arnold Weiss recalled how, as a thirteen-year-old Jewish immigrant from Russia, he was able to get his mother, who could not read Yiddish (the Jewish language), through the literacy exam. "For the reading," he remembered, "you faced the [inspector]. I was surrounded by an aunt and uncle and another uncle who's a pharmacist—my mother was in the center. They said she would have to take a test for reading. So one man said, 'She can't speak English.' Another man said, 'We know that. We will give her a *sidder* [a Jewish prayer book].' . . . I knew she couldn't do that and we would be in trouble. Well, they opened the *sidder*. There was a certain passage they had you read. I looked at it and saw right away what it was. I quickly studied it—I knew the whole paragraph. Then I got underneath [the group of adults]. I was very small, and I told her the words in Yiddish very softly. I had memorized the lines and I said them quietly, and she said them louder so the [inspectors] could hear it. She looked at it and sounded as if she was reading it, but I was doing the talking underneath. . . ."

However they did it, most of the immigrants passed the mental examinations. Some even managed to keep their dignity intact. "They asked us . . . 'How much is two and one? How much is two and two?'" stated Polish newcomer Pauline Notkoff. "But the next girl, also from our country, went and they asked her, 'How do you wash stairs, from the top or bottom?' She says, ' I don't come to America to wash stairs.'"

It was a defiant answer, but there was little defiance during the legal examinations that followed. Most of the immigrants knew that many of the questions they were about to be asked were potentially danger-ous—a wrong answer to any of the queries could send them back on the next ship. "Here is where the lies are told," stated a Department of the Interior report. "Most of the immigrants have been coached as to what answers to give. Here is an old woman who says she has three sons in America, when she has but one. The more she talks the more she entangles herself. Here is a Russian girl who has run away from per-secution. She claimed a relative in New York at an address found not to exist; she is straightaway in trouble."

The Russian girl was not alone in finding herself in trouble. Many of the questions were simple enough. What is your nationality? When were you born? But even here, there could be problems. Some immi-grants, for example, came from tiny, isolated areas where no birth records were kept. They honestly did not know when they had been

Since women were not allowed to enter the United States alone, the legal examinations were particularly hard on them. Here inspectors query female immigrants about the male relatives or fiancés they expect to show up to escort them into America.

born. Although this fact was usually overlooked, other issues were treated far more seriously.

One of the questions asked was, "How much money do you have with you?" According to an immigration law designed to prevent American streets from being filled with penniless newcomers, arrivals had to have at least a certain amount of money in their possession or they would be denied entry. The amount varied from time to time, but usually it was twenty-five dollars. A few inspectors were more lenient than others, and occasionally an immigrant with less than the required sum would be passed along if the official felt he was likely to get a job rather quickly and support himself. Most inspectors, however, operated strictly according to the rule, sometimes to the extreme.

"Does the law work hardships at our immigration stations?" asked a government report. "Yes, everybody admits that. Sometimes men are turned back for trivial causes. Four Greeks were going to Canada via New York. The Canadian law requires each immigrant to have twenty-

Immigrants suspected of not meeting the legal requirements were questioned by special examiners. This woman was trying to convince the official that she was legally fit to enter America.

  Q U E S T I O N S

five dollars. They had $24.37 each. When they found their funds short they wanted to come into the United States, but they could not. . . . A man and his son have had their money stolen from them in the steerage; they lack the twenty dollars and must go back. And so the sad tale goes on every day."

Sometimes, however, those who lacked the necessary money were helped out through the kindness of strangers. "You had to have twenty-five dollars on you," Ukrainian immigrant Jacob Lotsky remembered. "I didn't have it. So what happened to us, there was this mother with a little girl and I helped her out all the time. She says, 'Don't worry; as soon as my husband meets me, I'll get twenty-five dollars and I'll give it to you.' I said, 'Oh, you'll get all excited. You'll forget all about it.' I was standing there worrying what to do. Then her name was called. Her husband was downstairs waiting for her. She gave me the twenty-five dollars."

Later, long after they were in America, some immigrants would tell the story of how, after proving they had the required money, they would, while moving on to the next inspection station, secretly slip their cash to someone who lacked the necessary amount. "I can assure you," stated one immigrant, "that a certain twenty-five dollars were passed along from one passenger to another to help out those who didn't have it. And this had to be done with a quick motion of the hand."

Some newcomers also took advantage of outsiders who saw in the financial requirement a quick and easy way to make a profit. "Now in order to go through," recalled Emmanuel Steen, "you had to show your twenty dollars. But a little further back on the fence there were a couple of guys [who] would loan you twenty dollars. Cost you two bucks, follow me? And you'd go to the gate and come through the gate and the guy would be there to take the twenty-dollar bill from you. Cost you two bucks. For two bucks you could show twenty."

Surprising as it might sound, of all the questions asked during the legal examinations, the one that was most potentially disastrous for tens of thousands of arrivals was the simple query, "Do you have a job waiting for you in the United States?" In 1885 Congress had passed a law excluding all immigrants who took a job in exchange for passage. The law was enacted after it became clear that during the 1870s and early 1880s, many American companies were enticing foreigners to come to the United States by offering to pay for their passage in exchange for their going to work for the company. The problem was that once the newcomers arrived and went to work for their new employers, they were paid extremely low and unfair wages.

The law placed thousands of already confused immigrants in a bewildering situation. Any newcomer could be denied entry into America if an inspector felt he was unlikely to be able to find a job. Yet, he could also be excluded if he was certain of employment. Many of the immigrants had been told about this perplexing contradiction by crew members aboard the vessels that carried them across the ocean. "Remember," they had been warned, "you have no job waiting for you, and you paid your own way." But many of the immigrants could not understand what they were being told. And many of those who did simply could not grasp the logic of lying when there didn't seem to be any reason for doing so.

As they headed for the ferries that would take them off Ellis Island, each immigrant had his or her own special recollection of what they had gone through. Scottish newcomer Thomas Neil has his own unique experience. "The immigration man says, 'Where are you from?' he later stated. 'And I say, 'Glasgow.' And he says, 'What state is that in?' And I answered, 'It's in a hell of a state.' And he let me in."

Unfortunately for so many of them, the confusing law was most often strictly enforced during the legal examinations. "I acted not only as an interpreter but also as a primary inspector," Frank Martocci stated. "Sometimes there came before me a group all hailing from the same section of Italy and bound for a single destination in this country. . . . It sometimes happened that one member of such a group would produce a letter from a friend or relative within the United States to prove that work had been promised him here. He would willingly sign [a statement] of this, thereby leading not only to his deportation, but that of his entire group. . . . Once when I was the official interpreter, thirty-four common laborers were deported because one of them was honest about coming here as a contract laborer, and unwittingly involved all the others in his group."

Those suspected of being contract laborers were not the only ones to face a special peril. For just as the physical inspection had been particularly difficult for women, so too was a particular part of the legal examinations. Even if they had passed all the other inspections, unaccompanied women (and children) were not allowed to enter America until their husband or other male relative showed up to claim them. Officials were concerned that a woman alone in a place like New York would fall victim to people who might try to harm them. "If [a woman] had come to join her husband in New York or Brooklyn," explained Ellis Island interpreter Frank Martocci, "we could not let her loose on the streets of a strange city looking for her husband. Actually he might have been waiting [just] outside . . . for a week, but the inspector would detain the woman, and her children if she had any, until the husband came for her, for there were too many unscrupulous people preying on the ignorance of the immigrant in those days."

The men who came to claim female immigrants included those who had either advertised for brides in Old World newspapers or who had paid to have marriages arranged for them in various European countries. Sometimes the bridegrooms had photographs of their brides, but the women had no pictures of what the men they would be marrying looked like. In several instances a prospective bride, upon first encountering the man she was to marry, found him to be so physically unattractive or his mannerisms so unappealing that she actually asked to be immediately sent back home. But in most cases, a young woman was desperate to escape the horrible conditions in her native land and, in return for a man having paid her passage to America, was willing to take him on as a husband in order to stay.

Immigrant ships were so filled with prospective brides that, at first, inspectors required that the marriages be performed at Ellis Island as soon as a bride had passed all her examinations. Soon, however, with so many brides coming in, that policy was dropped and the marriages were conducted off the Island with an Ellis Island interpreter always on hand to make sure that the wedding took place. Fiorello La Guardia was one of these interpreters. "Often we interpreters at Ellis Island had to accompany couples to the city to be married," he later wrote. "We would take them to City Hall in New York, where marriages were performed in those days by [city officials known as] aldermen. The aldermen took turns performing the ceremonies and getting the fees."

The aid provided by men like Fiorello La Guardia in helping young immigrant women get married as a way of entering America was but one of the many services provided by him and his fellow interpreters. "As far as I was concerned, and almost everyone around me agreed," stated Louis Sage, "if it hadn't been for the interpreters we never would have made it through. They were the real heroes of Ellis Island."

Most of the interpreters were highly skilled in both linguistics and dialects. Many were able to speak between six and fifteen languages. That most of them had a sincere compassion for the newcomers was not surprising. Many of them had been immigrants themselves.

La Guardia, who would later become one of New York's most popular and effective mayors, worked at Ellis Island for three years while attending New York University Law School. Years later, in his autobiography, he recounted his experiences as an interpreter. "The work on the Island was difficult and strenuous," he wrote. "We worked seven days a week, for immigration was very heavy at this time. All of us were glad, however, to have the jobs, despite the long hours and tiring tasks. Immigrants were pouring in at the average rate of 5,000 a day, and it was a constant grind from the moment we got into our uniforms early in the morning until the last moment before we left on the 5:30 boat in the evening. . . . The immigration laws were rigidly enforced, and there were many heartbreaking scenes on Ellis Island. I never managed during the three years I worked there to become callous to the mental anguish, the disappointment, and the despair I witnessed almost daily. . . . On the whole, the personnel of the Immigration Service was kindly and considerate. At best, the work was an ordeal. Our compensation, besides our salaries, for the heartbreaking scenes we

FIORELLO LA GUARDIA was the son of a Catholic father who had immigrated from Italy and a Jewish mother who had come to America from Austria-Hungary. While working as an Ellis Island interpreter, La Guardia, who was fluent in five languages, earned a reputation as being one of the most compassionate of all the inspection station's officials.

After graduation from law school in 1910, La Guardia joined a New York law firm where he spent much of his time representing immigrants. He discovered, however, that he was more interested in politics than the law and in 1916 was elected to the U.S. House of Representatives. In 1933, just as the nation's Great Depression was beginning, La Guardia was elected mayor of New York City.

During the next twelve years, La Guardia became arguably the most effective and most popular mayor in New York's history. He guided the city through the woes of the Depression by securing millions of dollars in relief money from the federal government. Despite the hard times, he saw to it that scores of new playgrounds and parks were built in poor neighborhoods. Throughout his years in office, slums were torn down and replaced with public housing and schools, and many other social welfare projects were initiated. Largely through his efforts, many roads, bridges, and tunnels were built, transforming forever the landscape of New York. Included was one of the nation's largest airports, which still bears his name.

witnessed was the realization that a large percentage of those people pouring into Ellis Island would probably make good and enjoy a better life than they had been accustomed to where they came from."

Like the interpreters, most of the Ellis Island inspectors were conscientious and fair. Unlike the interpreters, however, it was they who, through their decisions, held the fate of each newcomer in their hands. Because of this, most immigrants regarded the inspectors with fear rather than understanding that when the inspectors acted with impatience or irritation it was because of the overwhelming number of people they were called upon to inspect each day. "It is all right to talk of kindness and consideration," stated one inspector, "but there comes a time, usually of overwork and the pressure of thousands of the waiting, when good intentions are disregarded, self-control reaches a breaking point, and the immigrants become victims. Unfortunately, they frequently try our patience beyond endurance. The only solution at such times is a vacation, which is exactly what we cannot take during the rush periods." Another inspector put it more simply. "We were," he exclaimed, "swamped by that human tide."

With the help of the interpreters, and despite their encounters with the inspectors, the vast majority of immigrants managed to pass the mental and legal examinations. Despite all they had been put through, it had been determined that they were "clearly and beyond a doubt entitled to land (to go ashore)."

With hearts lighter than they had been since the moment they had stepped off the ships, and with the official landing cards they had been handed clutched firmly in their grasp, they headed for the area where

QUESTIONS

Immigrants, all marked by their Ellis Island experience, wait for the ferry to take them into America. "Ellis Island," stated Russian newcomer Samuel Nelson, "was considered by everybody, by all immigrants, as a purgatory, something you had to go through. It's an ordeal."

the final arrangements for leaving the Island would take place. Almost all had been changed by what they had gone through, some in a way that they never could have imagined when they had left home. For, in many instances, they were about to enter America with a name different from their own.

Disagreements arise over just how many people had their names changed at Ellis Island. There is no question that the vast majority of immigrants entered America with their names intact. But many did not. The queries at each stage of the inspection process began with a

~ A COLORFUL HISTORY ~

T HE LARGE, SANDY EXPANSE OF LAND that became known as Ellis Island was originally called Kioshk (Gull Island) by the Mohegan Indians who lived on the nearby shores. In the 1630s, when the Dutch controlled New York, it was renamed Oyster Island to reflect the large oyster beds that surrounded it. When, in 1664, the British took control of New York, they restored the name Gull Island.

The most colorful period of the Island's history took place in the mid-1760s, when it was used as the site upon which pirates were hanged. In 1785 a New Yorker named Samuel Ellis bought the property and gave it the name it still carries. Ellis turned it into a picnic spot. After he died it passed on to his descendants until in 1808 it was purchased by the U.S. Government, which built a fort on the property. In 1867 the U.S. Navy used Ellis Island as an ammunition depot.

By 1890 it had become apparent that the government's immigration station at Castle Island, on the tip of Manhattan, was rapidly becoming too small to handle the task of examining the rising tide of newcomers to America. Ellis Island was chosen as the site of a new and much larger facility. In 1892, the Island was enlarged from its original $3\frac{1}{2}$ acres to 27 acres containing thirty-five buildings and a hospital. Most of the earth used to expand the Island came from sand carried in the holds of the constant stream of vessels that landed in New York, and from the hundreds of tons of soil removed during the construction of New York's subway system.

newcomer being asked to state his name. Inspectors would be told names like Vida or Sage or Moore. But they would also be given Gryszeyszn or Augerakakis or Zoutsaghianopoulous. Most of the officials tried to record the names accurately, but in the constant confusion that surrounded them and unable to understand what the immigrant was saying, inspectors sometimes took it on their own to shorten the name. Randazzese became Randa; Goldensternweiss became Gold; Perinowsky became Perry. Even first names were sometimes altered. Rolph was changed to Ralph; Margarethe was turned into Marge.

One of the most common stories later told about the name-change experience was that of a German Jew who became so confused by an impatient, overworked inspector that when asked his name, he answered, "Schoyn vergessen," the Yiddish words for "I forget." Thinking that the immigrant was stating his name, the inspector wrote down "Sean Ferguson" and it was with that name that the immigrant began his new life in America.

Whether they had their names changed or not, memories of the bewildering inspection process would remain with most of the immigrants all their lives. And for those who had been marked for detention, even more frightening experiences lay ahead. No wonder that years later, long after the inspection station had been closed, workmen restoring the facility as a national landmark found an inscription written by an immigrant under several layers of paint. "Why should I fear the fires of Hell?" it read. "I have been through Ellis Island."

An Hungarian mother and her children wait in detention for their husband and father who had come to America before them to appear at Ellis Island to claim them. For their entry into a new land, the mother had made identical dresses for her daughters.

CHAPTER 4

ISLAND OF TEARS

"The place was filled. . . . There were [people] who had been there for weeks and some for months, some as much as a year. And there was a feeling of desperation because we had no idea when we would get out and neither did other people." That is how fourteen-year-old Yugoslavian immigrant Paul Laric described the scene when he was ushered into the huge section of Ellis Island's Main Building where those being detained were being held. The detainees included those who were marked for further medical, mental, or legal examinations, those who required medical treatment, and women and children who had not yet been met by a relative or friend who could prove they would be cared for. They also included people without the required amount of money, men who had admitted that their passage had been paid for by an employer, and others whose status in being allowed to enter the United States was in question.

Difficult as the inspection process had been, it was in the detention rooms that Ellis Island earned its name "Island of Tears." "Oh, did I cry. Terribly," recalled young Russian detainee Fannie Klingerman. "All my brothers and sisters cried, so I cried. You don't know why you cry. Just so much sadness there that you have to cry. But there's more tears in Ellis Island to ten people than, say, to a hundred people elsewhere. There is all of these tears, everybody has tears."

For many, the tears had begun when they were first officially informed that they were being detained. With so many people being held back, the process was often chaotic. Interpreter Frank Martocci recalled a day when more than 1,700 men, women, and children were earmarked for detention. "I was one of the four employees whose duty it was to distribute . . . detention cards," Martocci remembered. "That day it took us all of four solid hours to distribute the cards to the 1,700 people, because added to the general noise in several different languages, we were simply unable to work our way through the massed crowd. We finally solved the problem by taking our places in the four corners of the room and distributing the cards by shouting out at the top of our lungs the names of the [detainees]. When they answered,

When he became Commissioner of Ellis Island, William Williams posted a sign in the employees' quarters that stated, "Immigrants shall be treated with kindness and civility." Here, children of detained families are treated to a play hour on the roof of the Main Building.

we threw the cards as near to them as we could and let them scramble for them."

It was a confusing beginning to what for thousands would be perhaps the most bewildering and frightening period of their lives. Waiting days, even weeks, for a decision to be made regarding their fate was often maddening. "At Ellis Island," stated English immigrant Ettie Glaser, "there was nothing to do. You could walk up and down among the crowds or wait for the man to come with chewing gum or an apple, but you couldn't go anyplace. . . . Even prisoners go out into the yard. But we were kept in a place that was all enclosed. I could walk up and down, back and forth, and up and down and back and forth. That was the extent of my exercise."

Some of the restraints were self-imposed. "My father was very watchful of me, because there were all types of men, all nationalities, all walks," recalled young Italian immigrant Marianne Riga. "My father had sisters in the United States, and when one of them came to visit he said to bring a harness to him the next visit. He put the harness on me and tied me to the belt of his pants, so that I could only wander a certain distance. That's how he kept me for the whole time we were on Ellis Island."

"In the case of aged people it was particularly pitiful," Frank Martocci stated. "You see, in nine cases out of ten, an old person was detained until called for by some relative or friend. At the Island, these poor unfortunates would wander about, bewilderment and incomprehension in their eyes, not even knowing where they were or why they were being kept. It was touching to see how, whenever they saw anyone who spoke their language, they would ask hopefully, 'Have you seen my son? Have you seen my daughter? Do you know him, my Giuseppe? When is he coming for me?'"

Along with the aged, another large group who were detained was young women waiting for prospective bridegrooms to show up to claim them. In these cases, detention officials were responsible for sending a letter or a telegram to the man informing him that he must come to Ellis Island immediately. Some detention officials were particularly sympathetic to young women who found themselves in this predicament.

TAKING A CHANCE ON MARRIAGE

THE CONSTANT ARRIVAL OF THOUSANDS of "mail-order brides" seeking to marry men they had never seen, let alone met, was a true Ellis Island phenomenon. Many came after being engaged by mail to men who had been put into contact with them by marriage agents in Europe. Others, willing to do anything to escape life in their native lands, took the desperate chance that they would find husbands once they landed in the New World, all the time knowing that if they did not, they would be sent back. On one trip across the Atlantic, the British steamship *Baltic* carried almost 1,200 would-be brides to America. Newspapers throughout the nation announced the date of their expected arrival, and bachelors from as far away as Michigan eagerly awaited the ship's docking to begin the selection process.

Newspapers also carried stories of the thousands of women who were being detained at Ellis Island while awaiting fiancés who might or might not show up. These stories prompted lonely bachelors, many of whom were newly arrived immigrants themselves, to write to Ellis Island officials informing them of their availability and their qualifications as husbands. "I am sober and use no tobacco," wrote a Polish immigrant from across the continent in San Francisco. "I don't gamble, am very loving, and have a happy disposition. I play the flute. I can make one good woman happy if one would wish to come."

Thanks to the help of these officials, many of the immigrants' problems did get resolved. Rita Alfano, for example, was a young Sicilian woman whose life had turned tragic when her husband suddenly died. Hoping to build a new life, she contacted a sister-in-law and her husband who lived in Rochester, New York, and asked them to sponsor her in America. When the relatives agreed, Alfano and her five-year-old daughter left their village, made their way to a port, and booked passage on a ship bound for New York.

Both mother and daughter passed all the Ellis Island examinations and looked forward to being released into the custody of the sister-in-law and her husband. But when they did not show up, the Alfanos were detained. After two days, with still no sign of relatives, Rita Alfano began to panic. She was all too aware that if no one showed up to claim her and her child they would be sent back to Sicily.

On the third day of her detention, the now-desperate widow, with the aid of an Ellis Island official, wrote a letter to her sister-in-law. "I have spent every day and night crying," she wrote, "racking my brain trying to find a way of escaping this hell. . . . What if they send me back to Italy? Oh, God, what should I do? I am here desperate with poor Fortunata who keeps on crying and asking when we can leave this place. . . . My dearest sister-in-law, I beg you in the name of God to send your husband as soon as possible because I can't stay here any longer. Please do not forget your unfortunate sister-in-law who has had so many troubles in her life and is now in trouble again."

The Alfanos were more fortunate than many other detained

women and children. Immediately after getting the letter, the Rochester relatives, until then unaware that the Alfanos had arrived in America, left for New York and Ellis Island. There they presented themselves and provided proof that they were capable of taking care of the widow and her child.

Like that of the Alfanos, most of the detainees' stories did eventually have happy endings. Many, however, did not. But whatever final decisions were made, the task of housing, caring for, and feeding the thousands who were held back was enormous. About 10 percent had been detained for medical treatment. United States laws dictated that

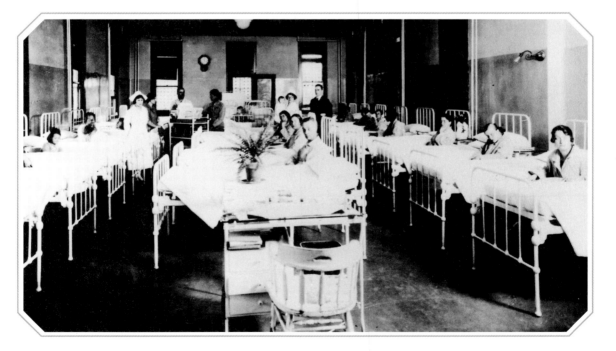

The Ellis Island hospital was one of the most medically advanced facilities of its kind in the world. This was the women's ward, where scores of different types of illnesses were treated and where many babies were delivered.

they were to be given the best of care free of cost. It was a generous policy, but one that was a most challenging task for the Ellis Island doctors and nurses who were often faced with treating Old World diseases that few of them had ever encountered.

The Ellis Island hospital was the largest medical facility in the world. During its more than sixty years of operation, more than 350 babies were delivered and more than 3,500 immigrants (including 1,400 children) died there. Dealing with all these developments while providing the best day-to-day medical treatment for thousands of patients tested both the skills and the devotion of the hospital's medical staff. Commenting on the extraordinary number and variety of illnesses that the doctors and nurses dealt with every day, one visitor to the hospital described it as "at once a maternity ward and an insane asylum."

Yet despite how overworked the medical personnel were, the story of Ellis Island is filled with accounts of staff members, particularly nurses, who treated their patients with kindness that often went well beyond the call of duty. "The nurses were there. 'Ladies in white,' we used to call them," recalled Elizabeth Martin, a Hungarian immigrant who had been hospitalized. "They were very nice. I mean, they talked to the children. They stroked their hair. And they touched their cheeks and held our hands. When they gave us milk . . . some nurses would kiss the child . . . they were really very nice."

Marge Glasgow, who had emigrated from Scotland, had fond memories of how a nurse had helped her get over the fear of being hospitalized while the doctors treated an eye condition she had developed on the ship bringing her to America. "I followed [the nurse] on her rounds, and she was very kind to me," recalled Glasgow. "She consoled me so much that I felt better. Then she put me to bed in a room next to her. The next morning everything was calm and nice. The nurse was still taking care of me. She took me outside to sit and see all the boats go by. I sat there and I wondered, 'Will they let me into [the] United States, or will they send me back? I so much wanted to live in [the] United States."

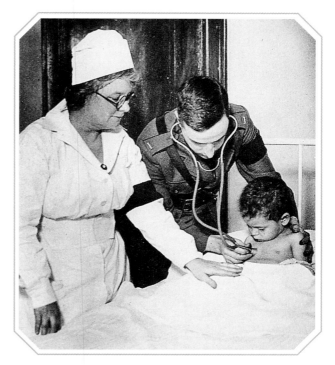

Of all the personnel encountered by those detained at Ellis Island, it was the nurses who, in the experience of many, were the most compassionate. "I had one nurse," recalled Polish immigrant Lillian Berger, "who not only took care of me but went out of her way to teach me as much about America as she could."

Dutch immigrant Doris Fagendam had perhaps the most heart-warming story of all to tell. "They detained my sister," she later related. "She had polio as a child. My mother made her dresses a little longer, hoping they wouldn't notice, [but] they did. But my father could prove that she would not be a burden to the country if they admitted her. So we just stayed overnight. . . . About a month after we were [in America] one of my sisters became ill, and the nurse came and saw my sister who was crippled and said, 'If you let us take this child to [Ellis Island] we'll operate on her and it won't cost you anything.' We couldn't imagine that, but they did. They took her. They operated on her. And she never wore braces again. She walked with a limp, but the braces were gone for good."

Most Ellis Island detainees were housed in several large dormitories segregated by gender, although children stayed with their mothers. At night the immigrants slept in double- and triple-decked beds. During the daytime the beds were raised and the dormitories were converted into waiting areas. The dormitories were always overcrowded and robberies were not uncommon.

Aside from providing medical care, the most demanding task that Ellis Island officials faced was that of providing three meals a day to the thousands of detainees. (In 1907 alone, 195,540 people were detained and had to be fed.) Just as Ellis Island's hospital was the largest in the world, the immigrant dining room, which seated 1,100 people, was the largest of its kind anywhere. Most of the employees who worked in the dining hall did the best they could. But continuously serving so many people, most of whom could not speak English and were anxious to be released, tried the patience of even the most sympathetic waiters and cooks.

"Oh, that room down there was full of people," recalled German detainee Agnes Grimm. "And then they brought the food along. You know, long wooden tables that went from one end to the other in the room . . . and they're pretty tough and rough, those people who work there . . . when you think of it, they gave you really, I guess, nice food. But the way they served it and the way they put it on, it was awful."

Adding to the difficulties was the fact that most of the meals

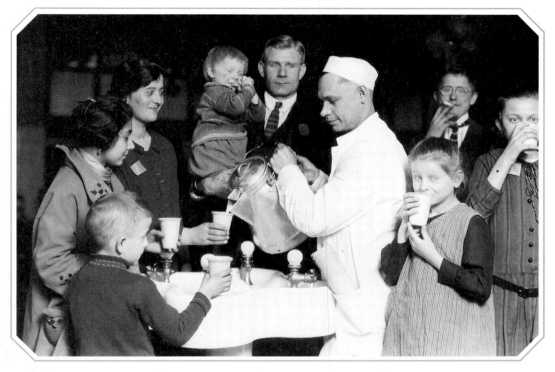

"There was a man who came around every morning and every afternoon, about ten o'clock in the morning and three o'clock in the afternoon, with a stainless steel cart . . . ," young Welsh detainee Donald Roberts remembered. These detainees were enjoying a mid-morning lunch.

included types of food much different from what foreigners were accustomed to. Scandinavians craved dried fish. Many Italians disliked potatoes. Irish newcomers could not fathom the mysteries of spaghetti. Perhaps the most challenging case of immigrant resistance to the food that was served came when a group of Mohammadan priests was detained. The priests belonged to a religious sect whose beliefs forbade them to eat any food over which the shadow of anyone outside their sect passed. After the priests spent several days refusing to eat anything at all, officials became concerned that they would literally starve themselves to death. Calamity was avoided when a clever dining-hall employee convinced the clerics that it was

GUARDIAN OF THE WESTERN GATE

ALTHOUGH THE IMMIGRATION STATION at Ellis Island became known throughout the world, another immigrant processing center called Angel Island served as the gateway to America on its western shores. Whereas Ellis Island was built primarily as a facility to examine newcomers from Europe, Angel Island was constructed to accommodate the entry of immigrants from Asia, mainly those from China.

The first Chinese immigrants came to America in 1848, seeking to strike it rich in the California gold fields. Because of deep racial prejudice against them, however, they were quickly forced to abandon their digging. In the late 1860s, thousands of other Chinese came to the United States, where they found work and proved invaluable in the building of the nation's first transcontinental railroad. During the 1870s, the nation suffered a severe economic depression, leading to outcries against Asian immigrants who were willing to work for lower wages than native-born Americans. In 1882 the U.S. Congress began passing a series of laws making it extremely difficult for Chinese to gain entry into the United States. This policy culminated in the construction of Angel Island, which was officially opened in 1910.

Among the tens of thousands of Asian immigrants who arrived at the facility in the next three decades were some 10,000 women, engaged to men who had paid their passage to America. Because the men had only seen them in pictures, they became known as "picture brides."

Although Angel Island was sometimes referred to as the "Ellis Island of the West," within the U.S. Immigration Service it was known as the "Guardian of the Western Gate." This name reflected its true purpose, for Angel Island was in reality a detention and deportation center rather than a processing station. For thirty years those who arrived at the facility were questioned and treated as if they were prisoners. Many were held for months and even years. Many others were deported. Some committed suicide. A poem written on one of the center's walls stated:

> There are tens of thousands of poems
> on these walls
> They are all cries of suffering
> and sadness
> The day I am rid of this prison
> and
> become successful
> I must remember that this chapter
> once existed. . . .

In 1940, motivated in part by a fire that destroyed the station's main building, the government closed down the facility. In 1943, with China a vital World War II ally of the United States, the discriminatory Chinese immigration laws were finally changed. Today, Angel Island, like Ellis Island, is a national landmark and museum. It stands both as a reminder of a dark chapter in the nation's history and as a tribute to the courage of those who survived the Angel Island experience and went on to build useful lives in the United States.

Feeding the hordes of immigrants who were detained for days, or even weeks, was an enormous undertaking. During the meals, most immigrants were introduced to foods they had never encountered.

all right for them to eat hard-boiled eggs since the shadows of "non-believers" had passed over the shells of the eggs, and once peeled, the eggs were free of contamination. For the entire time they were in detention, the priests ate nothing but hard-boiled eggs, which they peeled themselves.

Not all those detained, however, had such trying culinary experiences. Many were introduced to foods that delighted them. German immigrant Friedrich Pfeiffer and his family discovered whole new taste treats. "There was a buffet . . . and we right away steered for that buffet," he later recounted. "There were sorts of, oh, great big bowls of oranges, and bigger than we'd ever seen oranges before. It must have been the California oranges, and then they had pies there. We didn't know what a pie was. So my wife pointed at an apple pie. 'I want a piece of that . . . apple kuchen,' she called it. And then when she had her first taste, she shook her head and said, 'They forgot the sugar in this kuchen.' It was tart, naturally—as an apple pie should be. She felt they'd forgotten the sugar in that kuchen!"

Mrs. Pfeiffer's reaction to a food she had never encountered before was mild compared to that of Swedish immigrant Sonya Gillick, who, along with her sister, had been detained while awaiting the arrival of a male relative. Later recalling what happened when she first entered the main Ellis Island dining room, she stated, "Well, I went into this great big room, and there were lines of people. Oh, there were hundreds of people lined up. And I got as far as I could inside the door and I saw . . . they had these big, long tables, and men and women were [being served] big pieces of bread, and then each one had been given a bowl, and they filled it with red stuff. And I [went] back, and I told my sister, 'Oh, they're serving bread and blood.' I had never seen tomato soup in my life. 'Ooh, [my sister says] 'please we leave tonight and we go back on the boat.'"

Although her reaction to a food that she had never seen before was not as extreme as that of Sonya Gillick's, young Oreste Teglia from Italy was also mystified by a particular dish. "And then we settled at Ellis Island . . . we stayed there," she stated. "My sister took sick, I took sick, my other sister took sick. . . . I had a low-grade temperature and my eyes were red. I wasn't used to the electric lights,

I suppose. Different environment, you know. We got oatmeal for breakfast, and I didn't know what it was, with the brown sugar on it. So I couldn't get myself to eat it. So I put it on the windowsill [and] let the birds eat it."

It was not only new types of food that immigrants discovered during their stay in detention. There were other marvels as well—showers that gushed down gallons of water, toilets that flushed, and bed springs upon which children could bounce. Syrian detainee James Habjian encountered something that, to him, was truly wondrous. "I remember they had a big Christmas tree in

Thanks to the efforts of various immigrant aid societies and immigration service officials, many newcomers were first introduced to Christmas trees and Christmas presents while detained at Ellis Island. This photograph was taken on Christmas Eve, 1905.

the big building. I didn't know what a Christmas tree was. They had a gathering, a lot of people, and they sang Christmas songs."

There were other rewarding experiences as well. The same Paul Laric who had been so bewildered when he first entered the detention area discovered that all was not chaos and confusion. "My brother and I had met people our own age," he recalled, "and we mingled with them quite a bit, playing various games such as Monopoly and exchanging pictures that we brought along showing them what Yugoslavia looked like, and they showed us what various parts of the globe looked like where they came from."

Louis Sage also benefited from the three weeks he spent being detained. "When I arrived," he later stated, "I didn't know a word of English. But I kept listening closely to those who were speaking the language. I even met a new young friend from England. He taught me many words and phrases, and I did the same for him in Polish."

But despite all the new discoveries and even moments of pleasure, there was always the anxiety of what was ultimately going to happen to them. Greek immigrant Doukenie Bacos echoed the feeling of all detainees. "One Sunday . . ." he stated, "they brought, to entertain us, ballet. And it was a beautiful day that day. But still again, the pain was in me. I couldn't enjoy nothing, being that I was afraid they were going to send me back. And I was dreaming if they send me back, before I go to the . . . boat I'm going to fall into the river and die. I couldn't go back anymore. I had dreams. . . ."

Bacos's fears were shared by all the detainees but, most of all, they were felt by those who had received detention cards marked *SI*. The

Immigrants with their entry status in doubt pose with members of the Special Board of Inquiry before pleading their case. President Theodore Roosevelt, aware of the price that deported immigrants would pay, cabled Ellis Island officials stating, "We must remember that to send [an immigrant] back is often to inflict a punishment on him only less severe than death itself...."

letters stood for Special Inquiry. They indicated that the immigrants' eligibility to enter America had been put into question during the examinations. Specifically, an SI card meant that the immigrant would have to appear before the Special Inquiry Board, which would make a final decision.

The Special Inquiry Board was made up of three immigration officials. Arguably the most overworked of all the Ellis Island personnel, they reviewed a staggering 70,000 cases a year. Because of this, they tended to be lenient, and the vast majority of those they questioned were "cleared to land." Still, for almost every detainee, appearing before the Board was the most traumatic Ellis Island experience of all. "I was never so frightened in my life as I was when I stood before those men," recalled Lithuanian immigrant Abraham Krames. "My whole future was in their hands, and I could hardly keep my arms and legs from shaking."

In the end, 98 percent of all the immigrants who passed through Ellis Island were admitted into the United States. That meant that 2 percent were refused entry and sent back to their native lands. At first glance it seems that very few suffered the tragedy of being deported. But the percentages are misleading. Given the millions of arrivals who were examined at the island, 2 percent translated into more than 250,000 people whose hopes had turned into tears.

Many of those sent back were rejected for medical reasons, particularly those who suffered from trachoma or some other contagious disease. Others were deported for political reasons, especially if it had been discovered that they had committed serious crimes back home. Still others were denied admission because they were contract laborers. The largest number of those deported were sent back because officials had determined that they would not be able to support themselves in America and would become a burden to society.

Among the saddest cases of all were the women who had come to America alone claiming that a sponsor would be on hand to meet them. Sometimes they were rejected because their so-called uncles or brothers turned out be a fraud. Most often, their sponsor simply could not be found. "There were times . . ." reported Frank Martocci, "when

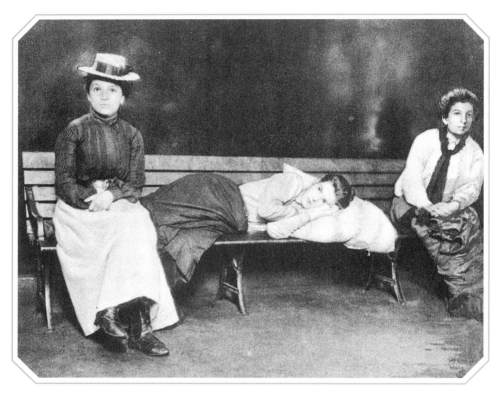

The saddest of all the scenes at Ellis Island was the sight of those who, having failed their examinations, were waiting to be taken to ships that would bring them back to the lands where their long journeys had begun. "I was powerless," wrote Ellis Island Commissioner Henry H. Curran. "I could only watch them go. Day by day the [ferries] took them from Ellis Island back to the ships again, back to the ocean, back to what?"

all our efforts to locate the immediate relative failed. Sometimes a married woman had come to join her husband, or a young woman [had come] to marry her fiancé, and the man could not be located. Perhaps he had died, or moved, or the correspondence hadn't reached him—who knows? In any event, the results were tragic indeed, as I well know from personal experience. There was no way of soothing these heartbroken women, who had traveled thousands and thousands of

miles, endured suffering and humiliation, and who had uprooted their lives only to find their hopes shattered at the end of the long voyage."

Most heartbreaking of all were the instances in which families were separated through deportation. A husband, for example, might have been admitted but his wife, suffering from trachoma, was sent back. A child as young as ten was found to be too ill to be admitted and was to be deported. This led to agonizing decisions: whether the whole family would return, whether one member would go with the child, or whether the child would go back alone. All too often, finances dictated the decision. The steamship company that had brought the family to America was required to transport the child back across the ocean free of charge, but they had no such obligation as far as parents were concerned.

With their dreams shattered and knowing the desperate conditions that awaited them back home, some 3,000 immigrants chose to commit suicide rather than be deported. Some killed themselves at Ellis Island or aboard the ships that were returning them. Many others drowned themselves in the dark waters off Ellis Island. And there were a number of cases in which those scheduled for deportation lost their lives in a futile attempt to swim from the Island to the mainland under cover of darkness.

"We were lucky," Italian immigrant Josephine Sorvino would state. "There were many who were sent back. And my sister said that some of them were jumping off the boats because they were told to go back, and they were committing suicide. Just the thought of that voyage going back and not being able to stay in this country. We were the lucky ones."

The millions of immigrants who settled in New York never forgot the sights they encountered when they first stepped into the metropolis. "It was," as one new arrival put it, "... all wild, all inconceivable ... [This] unimaginable city."

CHAPTER
5

STARTING NEW LIVES

"I wish I had the words to describe exactly how I felt when I went through those doors and was at last out of that inspection hall," stated Louis Sage. "I recall going down a steep set of stairs to the floor below, and all the time I was remembering that other set of stairs I climbed when we first got to this building and how frightened I was. I had my landing card in my pocket with my hand clutched around it. I never took my hand out of that pocket until the ferry that took us off the Island landed in New York. I still didn't know what was ahead for me. But one thing was for sure. I had made it through Ellis Island."

The stairway that Sage descended was one of three sets of steps leading down from the Registry Room. Together they were known as the "Stairs of Separation." Immigrants heading for New York took the stairs to the New York Room. Those heading for points beyond New York took the stairs to the Railroad Room. A third set of steps led directly to the ferry landing. The stairways also got their names from the fact that they marked the parting of the ways for many families and friends who were about to set out for different destinations.

No matter where in America they were headed, they all needed to stop at Ellis Island's Money Exchange. There they traded the gold, silver, and paper money they had brought with them from Europe for American dollars. For some, the process of exchanging money provided the final confusing moments of their Ellis Island experience. German immigrant Freidrich Leipzig had a particular problem dealing with American money. "One of the things that was hard understanding was the coins," he later explained. "In Europe all coins have numbers that show what they're worth, but in America no coin has a number on it. Show me where a quarter says twenty-five, or where a dime says ten, or where a nickel says five. Nowhere."

It was at the Money Exchange that some immigrants had an even more disturbing experience. "From time to time," stated inspector Frank Martocci, "immigrants complained of being cheated in the exchange. . . . One day an immigrant came to me complaining that he was short five dollars. Incidentally, it wasn't often that an immigrant

From the time they had stepped off the ships that had brought them across the ocean, the immigrants had been forced to stand in one long line after another. Even after they had passed all their inspections, other lines still awaited them, like those at the Money Exchange.

knew enough about the money to know when he was cheated. Another inspector and I returned with the immigrant to the money changer and asked him for an explanation. The immigrant, mind you, had just had his money changed by this man, who insisted he had given him the right amount. The immigrant insisted just as loudly—more so, in fact —that he had been shortchanged five dollars. Although I suspected the money changer, I had no proof and was about to . . . close the matter when the immigrant . . . after fumbling through his pockets again, reached over and pulled the missing five-dollar bill out of the money changer's pocket. It was done so cleverly that to me it seemed like [a magic trick]."

For those traveling to cities and towns throughout the United States, the next step in their departure process was to buy railroad tickets for their destinations. Once again they waited in long lines before reaching one of the dozen agents who sold the tickets. As with almost everything else they had experienced at Ellis Island, the ticket sales, for some, did not go without frustration. Just as the inspectors had often had difficulty with the immigrants' names, the ticket agents often struggled to understand where some of them wanted to go. An Italian woman, heading for Springfield, Massachusetts, told the agent that her destination was "Pringvilliamas." A German man, bound for Lincoln,

Those immigrants who were going to journey by train were able to purchase box lunches for their trip. Under signs that, in five languages, stated, "Provisions Cheaper Here Than On the Railroads," they paid 4 cents for a sandwich and purchased bologna at 13 cents a pound.

Nebraska, insisted that he be given a ticket for "Likinbra." A Hungarian woman, told by relatives to purchase a ticket for Second Avenue, Pittsburgh, presented the agent with a slip of paper describing her destination as "Szekenevno Pillsburs." The confusion led to long delays. Fortunately, the ever-present interpreters were on hand, and almost all the travelers eventually wound up with the correct tickets in hand.

After purchasing their tickets, the immigrants were given tags to pin to their hats and coats. The tags showed railroad conductors what trains the travelers needed to be put on and what connections they needed to make. With the tags in place, the immigrants then headed for the door leading to the Ellis Island docks. From there, they were taken by ferry across the bay to railroad terminals in Jersey City and Hoboken, New Jersey, where they would await their trains.

Meantime, those who were about to settle in New York City assembled in the New York Room. There, many of them were greeted by relatives and friends who had come to America, often long before them, and were waiting to take them to their new dwellings. It was a wonderful scene, the most joyous happening of the entire Ellis Island experience. Many of the reunions took place next to a post where long-separated husbands, wives, children, and friends hugged and kissed one another. For Frank Martocci, it was his favorite spot on the Island. "There is a post at Ellis Island which through long usage has come to earn the name 'The Kissing Post,'" he later wrote. "It is probably the spot of interest on the Island, and if the immigrants recall it afterward it is always, I am sure, with fondness. For myself, I found it a real joy to watch some of the tender scenes that took place there."

An immigration official places destination tags on a family that is about to leave Ellis Island and take a train to a part of America beyond New York. The railroad tags were among the last of a seemingly endless array of identifying labels that the immigrants had been required to wear since they had first boarded the ships back in their native lands.

Among the most tender of all the scenes were the reunions that took place between fathers and their children. Many of the fathers were men who, years before, had come to America alone and had devoted themselves to working as hard as they could so they could earn enough money to send for their wives and children. At the Kissing Post, many of these men met youngsters they had last seen as infants. "My father left when I was two years old for America," recalled Russian immigrant Katherine Beychok. "I didn't know what he looked like. I didn't have the least idea.... Then I saw this man coming for-

ward and he was beautiful. I didn't know he was my father. He was tall, slender, and he had brown, wavy hair and to me he looked beautiful. Later on I realized why he looked so familiar to me. But that's when I met him for the first time. And I fell in love with him and he with me."

Regina Rogatta had a similar emotional reunion that she would never forget. "My father," she stated, "came to meet us at Ellis Island. And when they called [his name he] came running . . . and he squatted on his knees with his arms outstretched, and the five of us ran into his arms, and we were kissing and hugging. We were so happy to be together. He said, 'We're all together now. We'll never be apart again.'"

They were together and, along with all the other newcomers who had chosen to settle in New York City, they were taken there by ferryboat. Here, still more alarming surprises awaited them. For, as unprepared as they had been for the perils of their ocean crossing or for what they had gone through at Ellis Island, the initial sights and sounds that greeted them in New York were, for many of them, even more shocking. To simple people from the country, the towering skyscrapers were almost beyond comprehension. So, too, were the elevated trains, enormous bridges, and the waves of people who walked the streets.

"We walked up Broadway, our father and mother in the lead and [we eight children] following behind," recalled new arrival William Reinhart. "And I saw the big buildings. We didn't have big buildings in Germany. . . . Then we got on an elevated . . . train, and all of a sudden, we were in the sky. Here we [had been] twenty-one days on the

The elevated railways that took many of the immigrants to their new homes in New York City were both frightening and awe-inspiring. Soon the newcomers would encounter the many other surprises, good and bad, that life in the largest city in the world would present.

water, and now we were sailing through the sky with water underneath us, which was the East River. I know I never stopped crying until we came down to ground level. . . ."

Young Scottish arrival Allan Gunn was taken by his parents to the place where they would live via another transportation marvel of the age, the New York subway. "Well," remembered Gunn, "it was scary . . . to go underground, and the noise—I think the noise scared us more than anything. And to us, being a kid, they seemed to be traveling awfully fast. And we wondered, how do you know where you're going underground? How do you know where you're going or how you're going to get there? Between the noise and the crowds, and being the first time you ever rode on the subway, it was scary."

Not everything, however, was frightening. "When I came to this country," recalled one French immigrant, "and I came to a pushcart on First Avenue, and I saw all these fruits and vegetables in February, it gave me such a lift. That I liked." "The city dazzled us," recalled a Slovenian arrival. "We had never seen such buildings, such people, such activity. Maybe the stories were true. Maybe everything *was* possible in America."

Like the Slovenian youngster, most of the immigrants had arrived with their heads filled with stories about what was to be their new land. One Italian immigrant remembered how, minutes after he set foot in the city, he spotted a group of men he was sure were fellow Italians, digging in the street. His heart leaped as he told himself that this must be one of the streets where gold could be had for the digging. Later he would explain, "In the old country, they used to say that America was a rich and wonderful place—so rich you could pick gold up in the street. And I believed it!" He was not the only newcomer who believed that story. For him, like all the others who thought the tale was true, it would not take long for reality to set in. As another immigrant would later state, "We thought the streets were paved with gold. Most weren't even paved. We paved them."

For millions of arrivals, the feelings they experienced on first entering the city were mild compared to their reaction to the places in which most of them would be forced to live. Almost all the newcomers were terribly poor and could only afford to live in buildings specially constructed by landlords anxious to take advantage of the hordes of people who were pouring into New York every day from Ellis Island.

The buildings were called tenements, and they were designed so that as many people as possible could be packed into them. Typically they were six stories high, lined up one after another with only a small alley between them. Each tenement was partitioned into tiny rooms, none larger than 11 × 11 feet. Most had no windows.

Up to thirty-two families were crammed into each of these buildings, and even the shortest tenement blocks housed more than 4,000 men, women, and children. In some of the tenements, as many as ten

A family poses inside their tenement. "It was so damp, so dark, so dirty," recalled immigrant Abraham Krames, "it's a wonder we survived."

people slept in a single room. Garbage facilities, plumbing, and heating were terribly inadequate or, in many cases, nonexistent. All the families on a floor were forced to share a single bathroom.

As poor and oppressed as they had been in their native lands, most of the immigrants had come from rural areas and were accustomed to green grass, sunlight, and quiet surroundings. Nothing could have been more different from that environment than the stark, filthy tenements and the crowded noise-filled streets and alleys of the neighborhoods where they now lived.

After just one week in her tenement house, Russian immigrant Anzia Yezierska poured out her heart to her diary. "Again the shadow fell over me," the young girl wrote. "In America were rooms without sunlight; rooms to sleep in, to eat in, to cook in, but without sunshine. . . . Could I be satisfied with just a place to sleep in and eat in, and a door to shut people out, to take the place of sunlight? Or would I always need the sunlight to be happy? And where was there a place in America for me to play? I looked out into the alley below and saw pale-faced children scrambling in the gutter. 'Where is America?' cried my heart."

The alleys about which Yezierska wrote were as much a part of the immigrants' new environment as the tenements themselves. So, too, were the streets. To avoid the dingy and crowded conditions of their living quarters and the oppressive summer heat, most immigrants spent as much time in the streets and alleys as they did inside their homes. In the streets they could gossip, exchange news from their old country, meet new arrivals, and share common experiences. They could also buy foods to which they were accustomed, clothing and other articles from the scores of pushcarts and stands that made each neighborhood street seem like an Old World marketplace. The streets also became the playgrounds of the children, who invented many kinds of games. Youngsters gathered around organ grinders and their monkeys. They listened to other street musicians and found fun in begging samples from the icemen in summer and the hot potato and chestnut stands in fall and winter.

From the time they arrived in New York, the immigrants learned that not only were the streets not paved with gold, but that finding a job so that they could support themselves and their families was

The alleys and streets of the tenement districts became the playgrounds of the immigrant children. Here, smaller youngsters look on as older boys play their newly discovered game of baseball.

extremely difficult. Most were severely hampered by the fact that they could not speak English. Thousands of others fell victim to the prejudices held by employers who were disturbed by their foreign mannerisms and ways of dress. Native-born workers, fearful of losing their own jobs to the newcomers, also made life difficult by openly speaking out against the hiring of immigrant workers.

Desperate to earn money, thousands of arrivals went to work in small factories, called sweatshops, in New York's garment district. There they were forced to work long hours for little pay. As one sweatshop owner admitted, "These [foreigners] cannot speak English and don't know where to go, and they just came from the old country, and I let them work hard, like the devil, for less wages."

Thousands of other immigrants made a meager living by turning their tenement apartments into "home sweatshops" where they took

Immigrant children quickly discovered that no matter how poor their families were, there was fun to be had with other newly arrived youngsters. Games such as leapfrog were particularly popular.

in what was called piecework. Entire families, working together in a single room, sewed garments, put together artificial flowers, assembled cheap jewelry, or rolled cigars. A young Sicilian immigrant had vivid recollections of long days and evenings in which his family assembled lapel pins in their tiny tenement apartment. "What you had to do," he recalled, "was to glue tiny artificial diamonds in the holes on the lapel pin. After supper my mother would clean the table, take the glass protectors off the wheels of the furniture, and pour some glue in each glass coaster. It smelled like nail-polish remover and gasoline. . . . Then my

Even the youngest children, like these shown here, spent long hours inside their tenements doing what was called piecework. "The kindergartners," wrote reformer John Spargo, "are robbed to provide baby slaves. What can four-year-old babies do? A hundred things when they are driven to it."

LET THE CHILDREN BE CHILDREN

IN THE EARLY 1900s, American workers were turning the nation into the envy of the world, and at least half of these workers were immigrants. But there was a dark side to the nation's immigrant labor force. Stricken by poverty, thousands of immigrant parents were forced to send their young children out to work full-time in order to help the family survive. Nearly two million youngsters age six to fourteen worked ten hours a day or more in the nation's factories, mines, quarries, and canneries.

In 1907 the National Child Labor Committee, seeking reform, mounted a campaign aimed at persuading Congress to pass anti–child labor laws. Impressed by pictures that photographer Lewis Hine had taken of immigrants landing at Ellis Island, the committee hired him to compile a photographic record of child-labor practices. For the next ten years Hine hauled his heavy equipment throughout the nation, capturing thousands of images of youngsters working amid huge, dangerous textile machinery. He witnessed them struggling miles underground in the lung-destroying atmosphere of the coal mines and laboring in canneries where sharp clam and oyster shells continually cut through young fingers.

When Hine's documentation was complete, the committee presented the photographs to key members of Congress. In 1916, thanks in great measure to the pictures, Congress passed the first of several acts that set a minimum age for workers and a maximum age for the number of hours youngsters under sixteen could work.

Millions of Jewish immigrants, many of them from Russia, settled in New York City's East Side. "Was this the America we sought?" asked one of these newcomers. "Or was it only a circle that we had traveled, with a Jewish ghetto at its beginning and its end?"

S T A R T I N G

father brought the lapel pins and spilled them on the table. They made a huge pile. . . . We'd work until midnight but never after one. At least I wouldn't, for I had to go to school in the morning. Yet sometimes I would hear my mother get up because she could not sleep [knowing the more pins we put together, the more we got paid]. And then my father would holler at her, 'Bimbabita, you will kill yourself,' and my mother would answer 'Sh-hhh, the children are sleeping.'"

One can only imagine how tired the Sicilian boy was as he dragged himself off to school each day after working on lapel pins until after midnight. But one of the main reasons so many of the immigrants had come to America was to build better lives for their children than they had experienced. And, as they settled into the harsh realities of city life, most realized that education would give their children their best chance for success.

In most Old World countries, there was no such thing as free public education, and only the wealthy could afford to send their youngsters to school. But in America, things were different. Schoolroom doors were open to all the immigrant children as well as to the sons and daughters of parents who were native-born. "A little girl from across the alley came and offered to [take] us to school," wrote Mary Antin. "This child who had never seen us till yesterday, who could not pronounce our names . . . was able to offer us the freedom of the schools. . . . No applications made, no questions asked, no examinations . . . no fees. The doors stood open for every one of us. The smallest child could show us the way. . . . Father himself conducted us to school. He would not have delegated that mission to the President of

ONE OF THE GREAT TRAGEDIES of life in the tenements in the late 1800s and early 1900s was that thousands of immigrant children were driven from their homes by poverty and forced to live by their wits on the streets of New York.

In order to survive, several thousand of the homeless youngsters became newsboys, or "newsies," as they were called. Many were as young as six years old. They bought their papers from newspaper dealers and lost money on any they did not sell. Commenting on the situation, New York Congressman James B. McCabe wrote, "There are 10,000 children living on the streets of New York. . . . The newsboys constitute an important division of this army of homeless children. You see them everywhere. . . . They rend the air and deafen you with their shrill cries. They surround you on the sidewalk and almost force you to buy their papers. They are ragged and dirty. Some have no coats, no shoes, and no hat."

Deeply concerned about the newsies, several reform organizations, such as the Children's Aid Society, were formed. The greatest help came from Father John C. Drumgoole, an Irish immigrant, who raised enough money to purchase a farm that became the largest child-care institution in the United States. He also established a vocational school for homeless children. Yet despite these and other reform efforts, the plight of the newsboys remained a national disgrace until well into the 1920s.

the United States. He had awaited the day with impatience equal to mine. . . . I think [the teacher] guessed what my father's best English could not convey. I think she [saw] that by the simple act of delivering our school certificates to her he took possession of America."

As each new wave of immigrants passed through Ellis Island, there was a growing awareness that learning to read, write, and speak English, and to understand American ways, was the path to real opportunity. Increasingly, even many young people who had been forced to take full-time jobs in order to help support their families found ways to get an American education. Sadie Frowne was a young Polish immigrant who worked six days a week in a New York City sweatshop where she ran a machine that made ladies' shirts. "The machines go like mad all day, because the faster you work, the more money you get," she told a reporter who interviewed her for *The Independent* magazine. "Sometimes in my haste I get my finger caught, and the needle goes right through it. . . . I bind the finger up with a piece of cotton and go on working. We all have accidents like that. . . . For the last two winters I have been going to night school. I have learned reading, writing, and arithmetic. I can read quite well in English now, and I look at the newspapers every day. I read English books, too, sometimes. I am going back to night school again this winter. Plenty of my friends are there. . . . Like me, they did not have a chance to learn anything in the old country. It is good to have an education; it makes you feel higher. . . ."

As the immigrant children progressed from grade to grade, they became fluent in English. By associating with native-born classmates,

Immigrant children at a public school in New York City's tenement district pledge allegiance to the flag of their new country. The pledge of allegiance was first recited in the nation's schools in 1892, the year that Ellis Island first opened its doors.

they also became streetwise in American ways. A great many parents, however, never learned English. And many refused to give up their Old World types of clothing and hairstyles. "It is so hard for me to admit, but I got to a point where I was actually ashamed of my parents," recalled Polish immigrant Abraham Krames. "They spoke such broken English, only a few words really. My father refused to get a haircut and he wore his beard down to his waist the way he did back in the old country. It was a terrible thing to be ashamed of people who risked so much for my sake. But I wanted to impress my friends. I wanted them to believe that I was one of them, a real American."

It wasn't just their lack of English or their Old World ways that hampered many immigrant parents and grandparents. They simply did not know how to deal with people or institutions outside their own neighborhoods. Gradually, in many families the children took over. In these immigrant homes it was the children who carried out tasks and even made decisions usually reserved for adult members of the family. "I was the one who always went down to the coal company to complain about the bill," recalled one Italian youngster. "And I was the one who dealt with the landlord. I could read the bills and the contracts and I could speak English to these people. I became, in a very real sense, the junior father of the family."

The Jewish newspaper column *Bintel Brief*, read by Jews throughout New York, put it more simply. "In America," the column concluded, "the children bring up the parents." It was an extraordinary development. But as those who had chosen to live in New York would continue to discover, it was all part of the bewildering experience of beginning a new life in a strange new place.

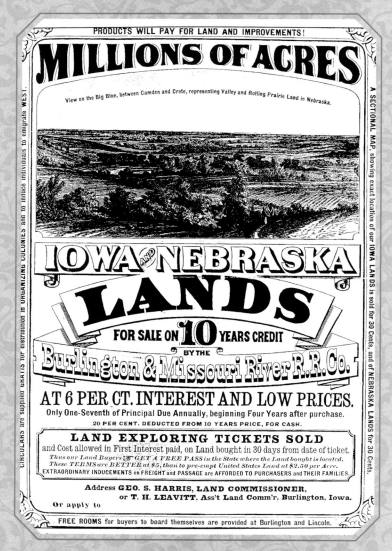

By 1900 more than half of Nebraska's residents were immigrants. Most of the other territories in the West had a similar proportion of settlers from foreign lands. Many of these immigrant pioneers had been drawn to the West by ads such as this one, placed by the railroad companies anxious to sell western lands they owned.

CHAPTER 6

BUILDING AMERICA

About one third of all the immigrants who passed through Ellis Island went to live in New York City. Two thirds chose to settle in other parts of the country. Among them were the millions who, once in America, journeyed halfway across the continent, determined to start their new life on the vast American plains.

Most of the immigrants who chose to build new lives in the West had been farmers in their native countries. Farming was in their blood and working the soil was all they knew.

Thousands were from Scandinavian countries—Norway, Sweden, Denmark, and Finland. Many others were from Germany and Russia. Smaller numbers came from France, Holland, Belgium, and Greece. A large portion worked from dawn to dusk for the meager wages paid by harsh landlords. All yearned to own their own land; most were aware that in the Old World it was an impossible dream.

But in America things were different. The U.S. government, committed to encouraging the settlement of the West, at first offered large tracts of free land to anyone who would settle on the acreage and improve it by farming. Even after the free land ran out, American railroad companies, anxious to build ridership over their expanding network of rails in the West, put up millions of acres of land for sale at extremely low prices. "No wonder," exclaimed French author and traveler Alexis de Tocqueville, "that so many Europeans who have never been able to say that . . . a portion of land was theirs cross the Atlantic to realize that happiness."

Happiness was indeed what they sought. But just as the newcomers who settled in New York City were immediately confronted with strange and alarming sights and sounds, so too were the immigrant pioneers. This was particularly true for those newcomers who, like Dutch immigrant Engbertus van der Veen and his family, had lived all their lives in Old World cities. After an arduous journey westward, the family arrived in Michigan in the middle of the night. "The moaning sounds of the western pine," van der Veen later wrote, "the night bird's shrill, weird cries, the hoots of the owls, the squeaking of birds and croaks of the insects throughout the woods, made a painful

Siberian immigrants pose near the train that brought them to their new home in the West. "You can see as far as you please here, and almost every foot in sight can be plowed," one newcomer would write to the relatives he had left behind in the old country.

impression on us who had come from Amsterdam, and filled us with dismay."

As alarming as their first encounter with the prairie was, and as inexperienced as almost all of them were in starting farms from scratch, most of the immigrants who chose to settle on the plains would eventually succeed in building better lives than they had had in the Old World. Fortunately the prairie soil was among the most fertile in the world. Fortunate also was the fact that all who passed through Ellis Island did so after farm machinery was introduced into the West.

For the immigrants, the horse-drawn planting and harvesting machines, like the prairie itself, were also something new and startling to be mastered. "Even the farmwork was new to me—something different from the work at home," a Norwegian immigrant later recalled. "Here [there were] enormous plains that seemed much too huge to harvest. And those labor-saving machines. Good heavens, such machines! I had to learn everything over again, greenhorn that I was."

Not all the immigrants could afford the farm machinery, and many of those who possessed the machines failed to survive the harsh challenges of life on the plains. For whether they eventually prospered or barely earned a living, every family was forced to endure hardships that neither they nor the immigrants who chose to settle in the cities of the East could ever have imagined. Most of these hardships were the result of the brutalities of nature that were particular to the plains. During the summer, searing heat and long periods without rain threatened every crop. In the winter, blizzards that went on for days put the lives of humans and livestock in peril.

One of the greatest dangers was the threat of that phenomenon of the plains known as a prairie fire. Almost every western immigrant experienced the shock of suddenly seeing a long band of glowing red light on the distant horizon. The shock would quickly turn into horror as the settler realized that the glow was from a prairie fire and that its flames, fanned by the constant wind, were racing at incredible speed across the dry prairie grass toward him, his family, and his farm.

"The fire," recalled one pioneer, "moved faster than a horse can run." "By its light," exclaimed another settler, "we could read fine print for $1/2$ mile or more." Other descriptions were even more vivid. "Soon fire began to kindle wider and rise higher from the long grass," wrote one traveler in Iowa. "The [wind] increased to stronger currents and soon formed the . . . blaze into a fire of torrent flames . . . blazing from earth to heaven. Dark clouds of crimson smoke curled away and aloft till they nearly obscured stars and moon, while the rushing, crashing sounds, like thunders, were deafening. Danger, death, glared all around; it screamed for victims. . . ."

A prairie fire was not only frightening, it was often devastating. After the flames had spent themselves, there was usually nothing left in their wake but the black surface of the earth. "We have heard," reported the editor of an Iowa newspaper, "of several who have lost not only the fruits of their entire labor, but also their house and stables,

As immigrants who chose to settle in the West were transported by train to their new homes, they encountered sights most had never witnessed. Among the most startling was a prairie fire roaring out of control.

thus leaving them without shelter and their herds of cattle without [food] for the coming winter. Houses can be rebuilt, but the season is far too spent [for replanting]."

The danger of prairie fire was bad enough, but there was another menace of the plains that continually threatened the immigrants' crops. The tall, lush prairie grass attracted millions of grasshoppers. With their enormous appetites, the insects, also known as locusts, ate every growing thing in sight. Within minutes, crops that a family had been nurturing for a year could be entirely destroyed. "I suppose you would like to know if we have been grasshoppered again," wrote Norwegian immigrant Mattie Oblinger to relatives in the East. "They were here several days pretty thick and injured the corn considerable. Some fields they stripped the blades all off. . . . They nibbled the ends of almost all the ears and ate all the silks. . . . [We] would have had a splendid corn crop if the hoppers had stayed away. . . . They ate nearly all my cabbage. . . . They left eggs here by the millions, so we do not know what damage they will do. . . ."

Russian immigrant Nickolai Berg had his own unforgettable experience. "One day when we were hewing [cutting] logs, there was fine sunshine," he wrote. "Suddenly the sun became darkened. . . . Shortly, a great swarm of mountain locusts descended. It appeared like the greatest snowstorms, and the locusts were exceedingly greedy. We had a patch of potatoes in bloom. . . . These were all devoured by the locusts, and only the stalks remained standing. They were so numerous down at the stream that they would bend the willow branches down to the water. . . . They visited us for three days. . . . Soon, they all rose, and the

"You would be so proud of what we've accomplished here," a Kansas immigrant wrote to his father back in Sweden. "We all work very hard and even little Seth helps out."

sun was all darkened again....The sound of their wings was as the burning of much stubble in high wind. They moved southward."

In his reminiscences, Nikolai Berg also told of another insect that, while not being destructive to crops, was a constant hindrance. "Mosquitoes," Berg reported, "were so numerous that we had to use smoke pots to keep them away both day and night. At times there was no use trying to milk a cow unless the smoke covered both cow and milker. When on the road with a team of horses, we would have to zigzag in order to have a slight wind facing the team or a side wind. When stopping the team, one would have to hurry down, because the horses would be covered instantly by pests. We would stroke our hands across the horses' backs and mash the mosquitoes. Our hand would become stained with blood."

Blizzard and drought, as well as prairie fires, mosquitoes, and locusts were all a part of the continual challenges the immigrants faced on the frontier. For many of them, however, none of these hardships was as great as the loneliness that came with living on the seemingly endless prairie, miles away from the nearest neighbor. "Mara, I have endured everything, you know that," Kansas immigrant Olga Stephenson wrote to her sister back in Denmark. "I've seen snow up to the roof, have almost drowned in mud, and have seen our crops eaten away by the hoppers. But nothing beats the [depression] that comes from being so far away from other human beings, so much alone so much of the time. I've heard of several women having been so overcome with the loneliness that they have taken their lives. I have no doubt that the stories are true. . . ."

The stories were indeed true, as were most of the tales of all the incredible difficulties the western immigrants endured. But these were people who had made it through the dangerous ocean voyage, had survived the ordeals of Ellis Island, and had endured another long journey deep into the heart of a strange new country. Their determination to succeed, no matter what the challenges, was as strong as their dream of freedom. For them, attaining success meant working as hard as the challenges demanded. Fathers, their sons, and often their daughters, worked hard all day at planting, harvesting, and raising livestock. Even the young children had important tasks, such as milking the cows and tending the animals. The work of the women was never done.

The women tended the house, cared for the children, cooked the meals, and, in many cases, made much of the family's clothing. Their labor was also often needed in the fields. And, like the men, they carried on no matter how tired or ill they might have felt. "My health has not been very good this summer," wrote Norwegian immigrant Laura Oblinger in a letter to faraway relatives. "The hot weather . . . made me so weak part of the time that I was hardly able to navigate. I was so

"A woman's work was never done," wrote Swedish pioneer O.T. Cardwell. "They never had any conveniences, and it is marvelous how much work they could [do]." It was not hard work, however, that was the greatest challenge for the immigrant wives and mothers. It was the isolation, the long periods of waiting for the men to return from the fields, and the loneliness in general that proved to be the greatest tests of their spirit and courage.

weakened down that, while stacking my grain, I came very near having a sunstroke. I felt myself giving way and got off the stack [of grain] and went to the house . . . and if it had been twenty steps more I would not have reached it without help, as I got very faint and weak. Everything turned dark, and my head got very dizzy, and I had to lie down in the door. Since then I have had to be careful, for when I get very warm I . . . feel dizzy and faint and . . . have to rest for a while. I cut 31 acres of a harvest with the help of [a] man I hired . . . and bound and stacked it all. I have threshed 14 [acres of wheat]." No wonder that the women came to be known as the "Madonnas of the West."

By the 1890s, when steam-driven farm machinery had replaced horse-drawn machines, most immigrant farm families became even more productive. Thanks to the new smoke-belching marvels, families who once struggled to plow or harvest 2 acres a day were able to plow or harvest more than 100 acres a day. In one of his letters, Uriah Oblinger echoed the achievements of many of his fellow Scandinavian immigrants when he wrote, "We are getting lots of rain [but] our crops began to need it . . . I will get 13 acres more broke out this season, which will make nearly 70 acres [having been planted]. I will have 32 acres of small grain to cut this season. . . . I will have 21 acres of wheat to cut, all small grain is looking splendid . . . I have walnut, cottonwood, willow, and plum trees growing on my place . . . I have 14 head of hogs and more coming. . . ."

Oblinger's accomplishments provided living testimony of how far many of the western immigrants had come since experiencing their first frightening moments in the West. Their lives were never easy.

An immigrant family poses in front of its South Dakota sod house. The "soddies" became visible symbols of the humble beginnings of so many immigrants who helped build America.

They constantly battled the forces of nature. They could not always get the prices they wanted for all that they produced. But they covered the prairie with the crops and livestock that helped feed the nation. They saw towns arise on the once-empty plains, and watched many of them grow into cities. In building new lives, they built more than half of America.

Theirs was a remarkable story, one that was being written throughout the United States. Thanks to hundreds of new mechanical inventions, the United States was becoming an industrial giant. The country's booming factories were supplying the world with manufactured goods. Skyscrapers, offices, and bridges were being built. From coast to coast, railroad and trolley companies were linking the nation with rails. It all required the efforts of millions of workers. And even though there was widespread prejudice against them, the immigrants' labor was sorely needed.

As American businesses, transportation systems, and construction projects continued to expand, hundreds of thousands of immigrants, including many who had begun their new lives in tenement- and garment-district sweatshops, found new employment opportunities. They were often forced to work for less pay than their fellow native-born laborers. Many had to relocate. And there was always prejudice with which to contend. But they found work, and in doing so, joined the ranks of those who, like the immigrants in the West, were building a bold new America.

Among the most visible symbols of American industrial might was the growth of the railroads. "We are fast becoming a nation endlessly and anxiously awaiting its trains," wrote a reporter for the *New York Times*. He was right. So, too, was the poet Walt Whitman when he described the trains as "type of the modern! emblem of motion and power! pulse of the continent!" By 1900 almost half the railroad tracks in the world were located in the United States. American railroad companies had become the nation's largest employers. And hundreds of thousands of these workers were immigrants.

In 1901 young Laura Corbin, who had come to the United States from Wales, took her first train trip. Later she recalled the scene in the New Haven, Connecticut, railroad station as she and her parents awaited their train. "Not since Ellis Island had I been in such a busy place," Corbin wrote. "Trains were pulling in and out. Long, loud whistles seemed to be coming from everywhere. A man with a very loud

voice announced each train as it came in or left the station. He spoke so quickly I could not understand much of what he was saying. Men and women perched behind what looked like cages were selling tickets to people standing in long lines. Porters heaped baggage in huge piles on large, flat cars.

"Mother kept telling me to stay inside the station, but father and I

"Here in America it is the railroads that build up the whole country," wrote a Norwegian immigrant who settled in Illinois. In many areas of the country, at least half of the railroad workers were foreign-born.

poked our heads outside the doors. Loud noises and huge billows of smoke were coming from underneath the trains. There were railroad workers everywhere. The [conductors] had very fancy suits and hats with badges on them. Other workers were in coveralls. They had lunch boxes and tools with them. 'They look so important,' I said to Father. 'They *are* important,' he told me, 'and you know what? Most of them started out in the old country, just like us.'"

Just as the locomotives became the symbols of American industrial progress so, too, did the nation's steel mills, where more than half of the steelworkers were immigrants. There they worked twelve-hour shifts, seven days a week. Andrew Carnegie, who owned most of the largest mills, gave his employees a day off on the Fourth of July. It was the only day of the year on which they did not work. For the rest of the year they labored day and night amid the enormous furnaces, which generated nearly 3,000 degrees of heat as they turned molten iron into steel. "Hard, I guess it's hard," stated one immigrant steelworker. "I lost forty pounds the first three months I came into the business. It sweats the life out of a man. I often drink two buckets of water during twelve hours; the sweat drips through my sleeves, and runs down my legs and fills my shoes."

It was often dangerous work as well. The final step in producing the steel was that of adding coal and manganese to the white-hot metal as it lay in enormous iron ladles. "You lift a large sack of coal to your shoulders and run toward the white-hot steel in a 100-ton ladle. You have to get close enough, without burning your face, to hurl the sack

This huge ladle, used to pour molten steel, was but one of the many enormous pieces of equipment that immigrant steelworkers dealt with in their work. "We made a living," stated one worker, "but we all knew that there were only so many years that we could do this back-breaking work."

...into the ladle and run, as flames leap to the roof...then you rush back to the ladle and madly shovel manganese into it, as hot a job as can be imagined," confided one immigrant worker in his diary.

As hot and dangerous as it was, the work went on nonstop. "We stop only for the time it takes to oil the engine," exclaimed Irish immigrant William McQuade, "a stop of three to five minutes....

THE PATRON SAINT OF LIBRARIES

ANDREW CARNEGIE WAS one of thousands of people from Scotland who were driven out of their country by terrible economic conditions and political oppression. Arriving in America desperately poor in 1848, he went to work full-time at the age of twelve. Despite his poverty and the discrimination he faced as an immigrant, he eventually built a steel manufacturing empire that made him the richest man in the world. Based on his own rags-to-riches story, he wrote many articles expressing his belief that in America anyone could become successful and rich through hard work.

Carnegie was a man of many contradictions. On one hand, he was often a tyrannical employer. On the other, he never forgot his immigrant beginnings and was determined to use his wealth to help generations of immigrants better themselves. In particular, he believed that it was the obligation of the wealthy to create institutions that would help newcomers to America improve their minds.

Before he died in 1919, Andrew Carnegie gave away almost his entire $400-million fortune to institutions of higher learning and the arts. His largest gifts, however, were reserved for libraries. Stating that "in a public library [immigrants] could . . . share cultural opportunities on a basis of equality," Carnegie funded 1,679 libraries throughout the United States and its possessions. To this day, millions of people have benefited from the generosity of a man who felt such a deep sense of obligation to his fellow immigrants.

While they are oiling, they eat, at least some of the boys; a great many of them in the mill do not carry anything to eat at all, because they haven't got time to eat."

It was not the type of life that most of the immigrants had envisioned when they had left their native lands, but it was the price they knew they had to pay. Determined to build better lives for their families, particularly their children, many worked so hard and so well that they opened new doors for their fellow newcomers. Philippe Lemay, who had first emigrated to Canada from France and had then come to the United States, was among the legions of immigrants who found jobs in the nation's textile factories. "It was a big event when I was appointed overseer of the One and Eight spinning mills," recalled Lemay. "There was to be a vacancy very shortly. I knew about it and, convinced that no one would say a good word for me, I decided to speak for myself. I asked the super [boss] if he wouldn't give me the chance. He was so surprised that he couldn't speak for a long time. . . . He was looking at me as if he had been struck by lightning. What! A Frenchman had the crust to think he could be an overseer! That was something unheard of, absolutely shocking. When he recovered enough to speak, he told me he'd think it over, turned his back on me and walked off. . . .

"The next day he came to me, and with a doubting expression still spread all over his face, said he'd try me for six months. . . . So I became the overseer of Number One spinning. . . . That was another step ahead for French Canadians. . . . I, a Frenchman, had jumped over the heads of others who thought themselves the only ones entitled to the job of overseer. . . . Later, several other French Canadian textile workers got well-deserved promotions."

Thousands of immigrant women also went to work in the factories, where they labored as hard as the men. Some, however, were determined to avoid the drudgery and harsh conditions of the mills. British immigrant Anna Smithson was one of many newcomers who was aware that, along with education, hard work was the key to success in America.

Women factory workers leave the mill after a long day. "We came over here with nothing but our bare hands," Italian immigrant Albertina diGracia would later state. "We were dirt-poor. This country gave us a chance to work and to get something out of our work, and we worked hard for our children. And now they've got what we worked for. We're satisfied."

"I got a job in one of the department stores," Smithson later wrote. "I worked four months at selling pins, needles, thread, whalebone, and 1,001 other items. Then, by luck, I got a better job as a demonstrator of coffee and teas in the grocery department of the same store. But I did not want to be a coffee and tea demonstrator all my life. . . . I began to take night courses in typing and dictation. . . . When I had attained the speed of over 100 words a minute, I got a job in an office at six dollars a week. Soon I got a job in another office at ten dollars a week. While I worked at this job I went back to night school, where I took a three-month 'speed course.' When I was done I got a job in a publishing house for twenty dollars a week.

"Here, all my studies bore fruit. Not only did I type and take dictation, but soon more important duties were passed my way. I even did some work usually reserved for editors. One day I mentioned to one of the editors some of the experiences I had gone through in working my way up from a salesgirl of needles and pins. After that I put my experiences down on paper, and to my surprise and delight they were accepted for publication in a magazine."

Determined, like Anna Smithson, to better themselves, other immigrants were willing to travel great distances to find opportunities. Henry Watson, from Wales, found his opportunity in a Wisconsin logging camp. "Ours was a large camp," Watson wrote, "at any one time there were at least seventy men working there. . . . The camp was divided into crews. There were choppers whose job it was to cut down the trees. There were sawyers, like myself, who sawed the felled trees into logs once they were on the ground. The skidders saw to it that the cut-up logs were hauled to the roads that led to the river or directly to the sawmill. Finally there were crews of teamsters who cared for the horses and were in charge of hauling the logs.

"We rolled out of our bunks at four o'clock every morning. At five o'clock we had breakfast and were at our work with the first rays of light. The work was hard and not without its share of dangers. The choppers were experts at dropping the trees just where they wanted them to fall. But sometimes a tree would crack and the upper part would drop straight to the ground, causing all who were around to scramble for safety. In the winter, frost and snow made the fallen logs very slippery, which resulted in many painful falls.

"Of the seventy men in our camp, more than forty were immigrants like myself. There were a bunch of Swedes, at least ten Germans, and some twenty Irishmen. Most, like me, had never even seen huge trees cut down in the old country. But we all loved being in the woods, and we all knew that as immigrants we were lucky to have work that we enjoyed doing."

As the American labor force became filled with immigrants, many of the newcomers succeeded in certain endeavors so well that they eventually became owners of some of the nation's largest businesses. Morris Horowitz was one of many arrivals who became peddlers in their new country. In a discussion with a government interviewer in the 1930s, Horowitz described how, although he personally never became wealthy, some of his fellow peddlers achieved great financial success. "How did I happen to become a peddler? When I came to Chicago, there was nothing else to do. I was eighteen years old. I had

The seemingly endless forests of Wisconsin and the Pacific Northwest attracted legions of immigrants who went to work in the logging camps, where they worked amid some of the largest-growing trees on earth. The goal of many of these immigrant loggers was to earn enough money to buy their own farms in the West.

learned no trade in Russia. The easiest thing to do was peddle. If you had a few dollars you could buy some dry goods and peddle.

"There was little rural mail delivery in those days. The farmers seldom saw a newspaper and were hungry for news. They were very glad to see a peddler from any large city. When I told a farmer that I was from Chicago, he was very glad to see me. You see, I was a newspaper and a department store.

"The farms were ten, fifteen, twenty, and even thirty miles apart. It would take a day sometimes to walk from one farm to the next. I used to meet peddlers from all over. It was not an easy life, but we made pretty good money. Most of the men had come from Europe and had left their families behind. We were all trying to save money to bring relatives to America.

"I never became rich, but many of the men who peddled . . . learned American business ways. Some of them opened small stores, which their wives looked after while the men were on the road. When the stores showed a good profit, they would quit peddling. Some of the largest department stores in the country were started by men who peddled with packs on their backs."

Most of the immigrants were forced to take up work that was completely foreign to them. Some, however, were able to earn a living through the same types of pursuits they had followed in the old country. Manuel Captiva, like his father and his grandfather before him, had been a fisherman in his native Portugal. In America he and hundreds of other immigrant fishermen settled on Cape Cod, where they were not only able to continue following the sea but played a major role in

In order to succeed, many immigrants, like this peddler shown with his young helper, took on tasks that were new to them. "All of a sudden, I started life new...," Hungarian immigrant Lazarus Salomon would state. "[It] was a different life, everything was different... but I never despaired, I was optimistic."

transforming the Cape itself. "I wouldn't never be happy without I had a boat under me," Captiva later explained. "In the old country we was all fishermen, me and my brothers. My father fished, and his father too....That's about all they do back there. I could work as good as a man by the time I was fourteen. I come over here when I was nineteen. The way I come, we had folks over here. My old man came over and my mother and us four boys. Then we sent for other people. That's how we all come.

"My boy's a good fisherman. . . . Me, I like to have the boy on my boat. Then I know where he is, what he's doing. The boat will be his. It's good for him to know how to handle her. On land, the Portuguese and Americans don't always get on so good. But we fish together all right. It's different on our boats. There's the same rules for everyone. The rules for a captain and crew are the same everywhere, and we all want the same things: a good catch and a good market. We get on good on the sea.

"We're the Portuguese pilgrims. We made Cape Cod. We built it up. Us and the American fishermen. . . . When we first came to the Cape, there wasn't nothing but sand and a few houses and boats. We used to dry the codfish on the sand dunes. There'd be pretty near miles of it spread out. . . . Then the artists came to Cape Cod. They must have painted [thousands of pictures] of nets and boats and docks. And then the writers heard about the Cape. And then the summer people started to come. But we started it."

William McQuade, Philippe Lemay, Anna Smithson, Henry Watson, Morris Horowitz, and Manuel Captiva were but six of the millions of immigrants whose labors contributed to the building of America. It was a contribution that did not go unnoticed. As early as 1908, in a speech to Congress, Senator Samuel McMillen stated, "Where would your great iron industries and constructions have been, where would your bridges and railroads have been, where would your mines have been dug were it not for the immigrants . . . ?" Almost one hundred years later, Lee Iacocca, chairman emeritus of the Ellis Island restora-

Those immigrants who came to America possessing a unique or valuable skill were among the most fortunate of the newcomers. Here, talented stone carvers who had been trained in their native Italy create an ornate stone panel. The panel then became part of the front of a building erected for use at one of the giant world expositions that took place in the early 1900s.

tion project, would explain what, to him, were the reasons why the United States became the envy of nations throughout the world. "It wasn't because of miles of open prairies," Iacocca would state. "It was because people broke their backs to till the soil. It wasn't because of a few industrial geniuses. It was because millions of people fired the furnaces and stamped the metal...."

The people to whom Iacocca was referring were the immigrants.

In honoring their achievements, he was also recognizing the extraordinary obstacles they had overcome, challenges that went beyond the physical hardships they had faced. For as one articulate Romanian immigrant had put it, "To be born in one world and to grow to manhood there, to be thrust then into the midst of another [world] with all one's racial heritage, with one's likes and dislikes . . . and to be forced to adjust to a new culture, new traditions, and new social conventions—if this is not heroic, I should like to be told what is."

Today, Ellis Island's Main Building stands beautifully renovated. Also awe-inspiring is the site's Wall of Honor, upon which are inscribed the names of thousands of those who entered America through the Island of Hope. As author E. L. Doctorow has written, "Ellis Island is the migrants' monument . . . with images of our ancestors fading in its shadows like memories of dreams."

ELLIS ISLAND TODAY

IT IS ESTIMATED THAT MORE THAN 40 percent of all American citizens can trace their ancestry to those brave souls who came through Ellis Island. The facility stands as a monument to the various ways in which they helped shape America. Ironically, it is a national treasure that was almost lost. At the end of World War I in 1918, the United States began establishing embassies all over the world. Prospective immigrants now went through their examinations at those embassies rather than at Ellis Island. The Island reopened as an immigrant-receiving station in 1920, and some 226,000 newcomers were processed that year. It then remained closed until World War II, when it served both as a detention center for enemy merchant seamen and as a training facility for the U.S. Coast Guard. In 1954, the last detainee was released, and Ellis Island was officially closed.

The Island was then put up for sale, but the government received no acceptable bids. Thieves began ransacking the buildings for furniture and scrap metal, and vines and grass began growing through broken floorboards and windows. But in 1954, the facility was saved when President Lyndon B. Johnson added it to the Statue of Liberty National Monument under the jurisdiction of the National Park Service. Congress, however, delayed appropriating the necessary funds to restore the facility, and it was not until 1983 that full-scale restoration began. In 1990, Ellis Island was officially dedicated as the nation's Immigration Museum.

WHAT HAPPENED TO THEM?

MANY OF THE IMMIGRANTS who risked everything to start life afresh would never find happiness in America, trading a life of poverty and oppression in the Old World for a life of poverty and alienation in the New. But millions, undoubtedly strengthened by their ordeals, would use their newfound freedom and opportunities to fulfill the dreams that had brought them across the ocean. For example:

Louis Sage, who told of how America was on everyone's lips and who was so alarmed when he saw the Ellis Island officials clad in uniforms, earned a high school diploma by going to night school and then became a successful jewelry repairman and civic leader in New Bedford, Massachusetts.

Angelina Palmiero, the young girl from Italy who had never seen a banana and had to be told not to eat the skin, worked hard, saved her money, and bought a dressmaking factory that employed twenty-eight people.

Amelia Giacomo, the young Italian immigrant who became frightened when a man told her that his eye had fallen out during the Ellis Island trachoma examination, settled in San Francisco and eventually started an import business that became so successful that she was able to sell it to the Hallmark Company for a huge amount of money. "I had a good life," she later told an interviewer. "The dreams of my parents really did come true."

Peter Mossini, who was startled to see so many bald people who had had their heads shaved because of lice, found a job on the Pennsylvania

Railroad. Later he started a sanitation business. After selling that, he built a bar and restaurant that he operated until he retired.

Jacob Lotsky, the Ukrainian immigrant who was able to enter America after a kind fellow arrival gave him the twenty-five dollars he lacked, started his new life by working in a dress shop. Like so many of the immigrants, he saved every dollar he could and wound up owning his own trucking company.

James Habjian, the young Syrian who saw his first Christmas tree while being detained, had to leave high school after his father died and his mother remarried and went back to Syria. He got a job sweeping floors in a photoengraving shop. Over the years, he worked so many hours that he was able to buy the shop.

Marge Glasgow, the teenager from Scotland to whom the nurses were so kind while she was in the Ellis Island hospital, began life in America as a maid. She went on to own two highly successful dress shops and used much of the money she earned to put her six children through college.

Doris Fagendam, the Dutch immigrant whose sister was able to shed her leg braces after being operated on free of charge by Ellis Island doctors, worked her way through college and then became a schoolteacher and later a school superintendent.

Edward Corsi, the young Italian boy who thought the New York skyscrapers he saw from the ship that carried him to America were mountains, spent his life helping other immigrants. Corsi's crowning achievement came when he was appointed Commissioner of Immigration at Ellis Island.

AUTHOR'S NOTE

WHEN I WAS A YOUNGSTER, my grandmother died and my grandfather, Louis Sage, came to live with us. He was born in Poland, had spent the first fifteen years of his life there, and because of this, spoke in broken English. I have to admit that I was embarrassed by the way he spoke, and whenever any of my friends came to our house, I always hoped that my grandfather would not be around.

Then, when I entered junior high school, one of the first assignments our English teacher gave us was to interview, if we could, our oldest relative. Reluctantly, I asked my grandfather if I could question him about his life. I was amazed by what he told me. I learned that, when he was only fifteen years old, Russian soldiers burned down most of his village and tried to force him to serve in their army. He said he ran away from the village at night and walked more than 150 miles to the nearest port, and used all the money he had to purchase a steerage ticket to America.

With great emotion, my grandfather then told me that his ship brought him and his fellow immigrants to a place in New York harbor called Ellis Island. There, he explained, they went through some of the most frightening moments of their lives as they were put through the seemingly endless physical, mental, and legal examinations. "Can you imagine," he asked me, "what it felt like to know that if you failed any of these inspections you'd be sent right back to the horrors of the old country?" My grandfather passed all the examinations and was allowed to enter America. Although at first he knew no English, he educated himself, became a skilled jewelry repairman, built a successful business, and put his two daughters through college.

When my grandfather finished his story I was speechless. Finally I said to him, "Grandpa, you're a real hero." I will never forget his reply. "I'm no hero," he said. "There were millions of us, and we just did what we had to do."

That is what I've tried to convey in this book. To me, Ellis Island will always be a symbol of the millions of men and women who, like my grandfather, risked everything they had to build new lives for themselves, and particularly for their children in America. As you've seen, I have told much of the story through their own words. If much of it seems remarkable, it is because what they did *was* remarkable. They not only built new lives, they also played a vital role in building America and contributed more than we will ever know to who and what we are today. I hope that I have done them justice. Most of all, I hope that what I have written would have made my grandfather proud.

MARTIN W. SANDLER
Cotuit, Massachusetts

FURTHER READING

GENERAL ACCOUNTS

Each of the following books provides excellent accounts of the immigrant experience in general:

Handlin, Oscar. *The Uprooted: The Epic Story of the Great Migrations that Made the American People.* Philadelphia: University of Pennsylvania Press, 2002.

Portes, Alejandro and Rumbart, Ruben G. *Immigrant America: A Portrait.* Berkeley: University of California Press, 1996.

Reimers, David M. *A Land of Immigrants.* New York: Chelsea House, 1996.

Sandler, Martin W. *Immigrants: A Library of Congress Book.* New York: Harper Collins, 1995.

Time-Life editors. *Immigrants: The New Americans.* Time-Life Books, 1999.

IN THEIR OWN WORDS

The following book is filled with scores of reminiscences of immigrants who passed through Ellis Island. It is particularly strong in presenting memories of what life was like for them in their native lands before they came to America.

Coan, Peter Morton. *Ellis Island Interviews: In Their Own Words.* New York: Checkmark Books, 1997.

The following book contains scores of interviews with the last surviving immigrants who entered America through Ellis Island.

Morrison, Joan and Zabusky, Charlotte Fox. *American Mosaic: The Immigrant Experience in the Words of Those Who Lived It.* Pittsburgh: University of Pittsburgh Press, 1980.

This brief book presents valuable insights into the immigrants' experiences in general, and the Ellis Island experience in particular, through their own words.

Lawlor, Veronica. *I Was Dreaming to Come to America: Memories from the Ellis Island Oral History Project.* Chicago: Scott Foresman, 1997.

PICTURE HISTORIES

These two books are filled with photographs, drawings, and other illustrations depicting the entire immigrant experience:

Chermayeff, Ivan. *An Illustrated History of the Immigrant Experience.* New York: Macmillan, 1991.

Handlin, Oscar. *A Pictorial History of Immigration.* New York: Crown, 1972.

STATUE OF LIBERTY AND ELLIS ISLAND

The following two books contain excellent accounts of the story of the Statue of Liberty. Both are filled with illustrations and, along with describing in detail how the Statue of Liberty was conceived, constructed in France, and erected in America, also contain interesting materials on the Ellis Island experience.

Abrams, Richard and Bell, James. *In Search of Liberty: The Story of the Statue of Liberty and Ellis Island.* Garden City, New York: Doubleday, 1984.

Allen, Leslie. *Liberty: The Statue and the American Dream.* New York: Statue of Liberty–Ellis Island Foundation, 1985.

TRACING YOUR ANCESTORS

This book provides practical information on how to find out if any of your ancestors entered America through Ellis Island.

Szucs, Loretto Dennis. *Ellis Island: Tracing Your Family History Through America's Gateway.* New York: Ancestry Publishing, 2001.

TEXT CREDITS

The majority of first-hand accounts in this book were drawn from the more than 1,300 interviews that form the core of the Ellis Island Oral History Project. Based at the Ellis Island Immigration Museum, it is the oldest and largest project dedicated to preserving the first-hand remembrances of immigrants who came to America through Ellis Island. Listed below are the names of the immigrants whose stories I used and the pages on which they are quoted.

10–11: Golda Meir; 14: Luciano DeCrescenzo; 15–16: Martha O'Flanagan; 18: Bertha Devlin; 18–19: Agnes Howerbend; 19–20: Angelina Palmiero; 22: Estelle Miller, Doukanie Papandreos; 23 (caption): Victor Tartarini; 24–25: Celia Adler; 25: Marge Glascow, Eleanor Lenhart; 26 (caption): Fannie Friedman; 27: Albert Mardirossian; 28: Anne Vida, Carl Belapp; 31: Clara Rudder; 31–32: Ljubica Wuchina; 32: Thomas Rogen; 32–33: Emmanuel Steen; 34: Rita Seltzer; 34–35: Peter Mossini; 35: John Peter; 36: Emmanuel Steen, Rachel Chenitz; 37, 38: Issac Bashevis Singer; 39: Amelia Giacomo; 40–41: Doukanie Papandreos; 43: Florence Norris; 47: Helen Saban, Arnold Weiss; 48: Pauline Notkoff; 51: Jacob Lotsky; 51–52: Emmanuel Steen; 54-55: Frank Martocci; 59 (caption): Samuel Nelson; 63: Paul Laric; 64: Fannie Klingerman; 64–65: Frank Martocci; 65–66: Ettie Glaser; 66: Frank Martocci; 66: Marianne Riga; 70: Elizabeth Martin; 70–71: Marge Glascow; 71–72: Doris Fagendam; 72: Agnes Grimm; 73 (caption): Donald Roberts; 76–77: Friedrich Pfeiffer; 77: Sonya Gillick; 77–78: Oreste Teglia; 78: James Habjian; 78–79: Paul Laric; 79: Doukenie Bacos; 81–83: Frank Martocci; 82 (caption): Henry H. Curran; 83: Josephine Sorvino; 85: Louis Sage; 86: Freidrich Leipzig; 86–87, 89: Frank Martocci; 90–91- Katherine Beychok; 91: Regina Rogatta, William Reinhart; 92: Allan Gunn; 129 (caption): Lazarus Salomon.

The following accounts were adapted from the interviews conducted by the Life Histories, Federal Writer's Project, 1936–1940. The Life Histories manuscripts are housed at the Library of Congress. 112: Mattie Oblinger; 115 (caption): O.T. Cardwell; 115–116: Laura Oblinger; 116: Uriah Oblinger; 123–124: Philippe Lemay; 126, 128: Morris Horowitz; 128–130: Manuel Captiva.

The accounts listed below were adapted from interviews conducted by the author in 1951. 7, 28, 30, 56: Louis Sage; 81: Abraham Krames; 85: Louis Sage; 94 (caption), 104: Abraham Krames.

The following first-hand accounts were drawn from unpublished manuscripts. 112–114: Nikolai Berg; Olga Stephenson; 118–119: Laura Corbin; 125–126: Henry Watson.

The following first-hand accounts were taken from materials in the following archives: National Archives – 93: French immigrant, Slovenian immigrant. Naylor Archives – 8: immigrant youngster ("We've lived through a famine . . . "); 20: steerage passenger; 51: immigrant ("I can assure you . . . "); 67: lonely Polish immigrant; 105: immigrant boy (I was the one . . . "); 120: immigrant steelworker ("Hard, I guess it's hard . . . "); 120–121: immigrant steelworker ("You lift a sack of coal . . . "); 121, 123: William McQuade. State

Historical Society of Iowa – 110–111: pioneer's account of prairie fire. Utah Historical Society – 8–9: Sophie Trupin.

Listed below are books from which some of the first-hand accounts in this book were taken along with the pages on which each account appears and an identifying reference to the person whose account has been included.

Leslie Allen. *Liberty: The Statue and The Dream. Ellis Island Foundation*, 1985 — 24: Italian boy; 34: new arrival ("I did not see any religious pictures on the walls."); 100 (caption): newcomer ("Was this the America we sought?"); 119: Norwegian immigrant. Jerry Mangione. *La Storia: Five Centuries of the Italian American Experience*. HarperCollins, 1992 — 11, 13: immigrant youngster going to the train; 68: Rita Alfano; 93: Italian immigrant ("In the old country they used to say . . . "); 97: sweatshop owner; 98: Sicilian immigrant. Mary Antin. *The Promised Land*. Houghton Mifflin, 1912 — 14: Mary Antin; 101–103: *Time–Life* Editors. *Immigrants: The New Americans*. Time Life Books, 1988 — 33 (caption): newcomer ("I was afraid . . . "); Joan Morrison and Charlotte Fox Zabusky. *American Mosaic*, University of Pittsburgh Press, 1980 — 53 (caption): Thomas Neil. Fiorello LaGuardia. *The Making of an Insurgent*. Greenwood Publishing, 1948 — 55: Fiorello LaGuardia; 56,58: Fiorello LaGuardia. Anzia Yezierska. *How I Found America*, "Story of a Sweatshop Girl." *The Independent*, 1905 — 103: Sadie Frowne. *The Bitter Cry of the Children*. MacMillan, 1906 — 98 (caption): John Spargo. Alexis de Toqueville. *Democracy in America*. Mentor Books, 1956 — 108: Alexis de Tocqueville. Engbertus Vanderveen. *Life History and Reminiscences of Engbertus Vander Veen*. Holland Sentinel, 1915 — 108: Engbertus Vander Veen. *Trang Vei*. Skardal, 1899 — 109–110: Norwegian immigrant. Walt Whitman. *Leaves of Grass*. Penguin Books, 1992 — 118: Walt Whitman. Arthur Williams. *The Long Day*. Century Publishing, 1906 — 125: Anna Smithson. Marshall Davidson. *Life in America*. Houghton Mifflin, 1951 — 132: Russian immigrant. *Jewish Daily Forward*, 1908 — 9: Italian immigrant ("If America did not exist . . . ").

The statements of the two unidentified Ellis Island inspectors (page 58) were taken from accounts in the collections of the Ellis Island Oral History Project. The statements of Senator James B. McCabe (page 10) and Senator Samuel McMillen (page 130) were taken from the publication *United States Congressional Reports*. The statements by Lee Iacocca (pages 130–131) were excerpted from his speech at the Ellis Island Family Heritage Awards in 2001.

PHOTO CREDITS

Catholic University of America: 88; Collection of Martin W. Sandler: 50, 119, 129; Corbis/Gail Mooney: 132; Eastman House: 28, 40, 73, 90, 96; Institute for Regional Studies, North Dakota State University: 117; Library of Congress: cover, title page, 6, 9, 10, 15, 16, 17, 18, 23, 26, 33, 39, 42, 49, 59, 82, 84, 92, 94, 97, 98, 100, 104, 106, 109, 111, 115, 121; National Archives: 24; Park Service, Statue of Liberty National Monument: 11, 31, 32, 62, 65, 69, 76, 78, 80, 87; Naylor Collection of Historical Images: 35, 45, 53, 71, 113.

INDEX